FAULKNER'S

As I Lay Dying

Title page of the original edition of *As I Lay Dying*.
Reproduced with the kind permission of Maurice
Edgar Coindreau, who translated the book into
French.

AS I LAY DYING

---

*WILLIAM
FAULKNER*

NEW YORK

JONATHAN CAPE: HARRISON SMITH

FAULKNER'S

As I Lay Dying

BY

André Bleikasten

REVISED AND ENLARGED EDITION

TRANSLATED BY

ROGER LITTLE

WITH THE COLLABORATION OF THE AUTHOR

Indiana University Press

BLOOMINGTON / LONDON

Most of this book appeared in French in Collection U₂, *copyright © Librairie
Armand Colin, Paris, 1970.*

Published in Canada by Fitzhenry & Whiteside Limited, Don Mills, Ontario

Library of Congress catalog card number: 72-79904

ISBN:
0-253-32150-6 (cl.)
0-253-20159-4 (paper)

Manufactured in the United States of America

CONTENTS

Contents

PREFACE

ALTHOUGH the volume of Faulkner criticism and scholarship has been steadily growing over the past decades, the number of published full-length studies of individual works is surprisingly small. At least two-thirds of the books on Faulkner published in recent years have been general assessments, surveying all or most of the novels, and while some of them are honest and dependable guides to Faulkner's fiction, few have added substantially to our knowledge and understanding of the novelist, and none can be ranked with those of Olga Vickery, Cleanth Brooks, or Michael Millgate. This is not to say that Faulkner criticism is presently at a low ebb, but that the authority of these three experts remains unchallenged as far as evaluation and interpretation of the writer's overall achievement are concerned.

What seems to characterize Faulkner studies at this point is a certain dispersion, and those looking for sound scholarship and fresh critical insights are now more likely to find them in journals than elsewhere. Yet essays, provocative as they may be, are necessarily limited in their scope. At best they illuminate the significance of a particular theme, trace a hitherto unperceived symbolic pattern, or reveal some neglected aspect of the novelist's narrative strategy. They can hardly be expected to investigate their subject in breadth as well as depth.

The prevalence of this fragmentary approach and the concomitant failure to produce new general studies of enduring interest probably correspond to a necessary phase in Faulkner criticism. The time has not yet come for a systematic and thorough reevaluation of the whole of Faulkner's fiction, and such a task will obviously require both patient scholarship and acute critical intelligence. Meanwhile, much is to be done, many areas of Faulkner's work are still unexplored and uncharted, and before indulging in further speculations upon ultimate meanings, it would perhaps be wise to return to his novels and give each of them the close and sustained attention it deserves.

The present study is a modest attempt to do precisely this for *As I Lay Dying*. My reasons for choosing this novel are easy to explain: being one of Faulkner's best books, it certainly merits careful scrutiny, but as it is also one of his shorter works and has provoked less critical interest than his other masterpieces, I found it less intimidating, less difficult to cope with than, say, *The Sound and the Fury, Absalom, Absalom!* or *Go Down, Moses*. My purpose in writing this study was to offer a comprehensive approach to *As I Lay Dying,* based on a close reading of the novel's text (from the initial stages of its composition to the final version of the published book) and on a detailed examination of its formal and technical aspects (language, style, structure, creation of character) as well as of its thematic design. My indebtedness to the whole body of Faulkner criticism and more specifically to previous studies of *As I Lay Dying* will easily be seen. Many of the latter I found helpful and stimulating, some I found useless or wrongheaded. I have made ample use of the findings of my predecessors while attempting to integrate them into a perspective of my own.

This book was first published in France in 1970 and was originally intended for French students of Faulkner. In translating it for an American audience, I have not altogether resisted the temptation of revising it. There are numerous changes in phrasing and small additions have been made in several chapters to clarify or qualify certain statements. The general pattern of the book has also been slightly altered and the bibliography has been brought up to date. But the main argument of my study remains as it was originally conceived.

In my work on *As I Lay Dying* and in my not yet completed

research on Faulkner's novels, I have profited from the encouragement and assistance of various people and institutions. I wish to thank the Fulbright and Smith-Mundt Foundations, which financed my first research visit to the United States in the summer of 1967. I also wish to express my gratitude to the American Council of Learned Societies for granting me the fellowship which enabled me to spend a year at the University of Virginia in 1969–70. My thanks are also due to the Alderman Library of the University of Virginia and the William Faulkner Foundation, for giving me access to the Faulkner materials in their possession, and to Mrs. Jill Faulkner Summers, for her kind permission to quote from the manuscript and typescript of *As I Lay Dying* and to reproduce pages thereof. Finally, I wish to acknowledge my debt to all those who gave freely of their time to read and criticize my manuscript, or to help me in preparing the translation: to Michel Gresset and François Pitavy, who gave my manuscript careful reading and made many valuable suggestions; to Dan O. Via, Jr., Michael Issacharoff, and John Donovan, with whom I discussed the translation and who offered many corrective comments; and especially to Roger Little, without whose prompt and diligent collaboration there would have been no translation of my study.

Strasbourg, May 1972

FAULKNER'S

As I Lay Dying

The only reliable edition of *As I Lay Dying* is the corrected and reset edition published by Random House in 1964. The corrections in that edition are based on a collation, under the direction of Professor James B. Meriwether, of the first edition (New York: Jonathan Cape and Harrison Smith, 1930) and Faulkner's original manuscript and typescript.

All quotations from *As I Lay Dying* refer to that edition (reproduced photographically in the Vintage paperback edition).

1

Introduction

ADDIE BUNDREN, a farmer's wife from the backwoods hills of
Mississippi, has just died, and in order to respect her last wish
her family undertakes a long and perilous journey to carry her
coffin to a distant graveyard at Jefferson. That is the story of *As I
Lay Dying*. It appears simple. But such a summary of the tale
leaves everything to be said about the novel. For what strikes us
immediately is less the story itself than the way it is told, or rather
the contrast between the tale and the telling, between the simplicity of the anecdote and the sophistication of the narrative
method. To make something of the pathetic, macabre, or comic
potential of his subject, Faulkner could simply have relied on
the proven recipes of traditional narrative. He chose, however, a
more adventurous and more difficult path, experimenting again
—as he had already done in *The Sound and the Fury* and, more
timidly, in his early novels—with new techniques. If, by its subject matter, *As I Lay Dying* belongs to the oral and literary tradition of folktales and tall stories, the novelist's approach to his
art is definitely modern. As in *The Sound and the Fury*, Faulkner uses here James Joyce's "stream-of-consciousness" method:
As I Lay Dying is presented as a series of interior monologues,
and each one of these, as well as relating a moment in the action,
shows us its refraction through an individual consciousness.

But instead of arranging the monologues in large, compact sections as he had done in his previous novel, Faulkner fragments them with seeming arbitrariness. *As I Lay Dying* surprises one straightaway by its utterly disjointed composition. In fact, only in the epistolary novel could one find precedents for such extreme segmentation, and the brevity of the sections calls to mind the scenes of a play rather than the chapters of a work of fiction. Hence an impression of discontinuity, which is increased on reading by the almost kaleidoscopic rotation of the viewpoints. In each section the perspective shifts, the lighting changes, so that each time the reader is caught off balance and forced to make constant readjustments if he wants to follow the narrative through all its twists and turns.

To these breaks in the storytelling are added the equally puzzling switches in tone and style. They also derive to a large extent from the mobility of the point of view, since whenever that changes, the story assumes the voice of a different narrator. Almost all the characters of the novel, it is true, speak the same rural idiom, and their monologues often have the familiar ring of a straightforward oral tale. But Faulkner is not content simply to exploit the stylistic resources of this vernacular for humorous effects, by playing on the naive vigor of its diction and on the drollery of its unorthodox grammar. Nor does he merely vary its use according to the personality and mood of the speaker. On the earthy base of this rustic colloquial prose, he continually traces the startling arabesques of his own rhetoric. The author's presence is particularly obvious in the lyrical outbursts and metaphysical reveries of Darl, whose style is virtually indistinguishable from the writer's own. It is also to be felt in Addie Bundren's terse, impassioned eloquence in section 40. Yet this richer, denser, more freely inventive style is not restricted to any one character: even in those whose linguistic capacities seem severely limited—in Vardaman, for example, or Dewey Dell—language sometimes takes flight, and from the most halting prose suddenly springs, by virtue of an unexpected metaphor, a poetic vision which transfigures it.

Small wonder, then, that *As I Lay Dying* embarrasses critics who are hard put to define its genre. In its style as well as in its structure and significance, this will-o'-the-wisp novel seems to elude all attempts at classification.

Is it to be considered as a naturalistic novel, as a commentary on the economic deprivation and cultural illiteracy of poor whites? Faulkner's Mississippi hill-country farmers have been compared to Caldwell's Georgia sharecroppers; the odyssey of the Bundrens has been likened to the exodus of the Joads in *The Grapes of Wrath.* Yet even though Faulkner gives realism its due, nothing was further from his intentions than offering his readers an objective portrait of a family of poor whites: "it does sort of amuse me when I hear 'em talking about the sociological picture that I present in something like *As I Lay Dying,* for instance."[1] Is it more relevant, then, to define the book as a philosophical novel?[2] There is no doubt that moral and metaphysical concerns occupy—as in most of Faulkner's novels—a central place, but such a label, apart from recalling the lengthy arguments of the novel of ideas, tends to overlook the fact that the language of *As I Lay Dying* is the language of fiction, and it tells us nothing of the specific nature of the work.

If one tries to classify it according to mood rather than content, the same difficulties arise, and only at the cost of oversimplification can one manage to fit it into a recognized category. While allowing provisos, some have emphasized its comic elements, others its tragic aspects, and still others would make an epic of it.[3] Does *As I Lay Dying* express Faulkner's "comic vision"?[4] None would disagree that the novel lacks the sustained tension of *The Sound and the Fury:* there is humor in abundance, from the most innocent to the most macabre, and in all sorts of ways—in the grotesqueness of several characters as well as the extravagance of many an episode—it could be taken for a country farce. But there is too much grimness in the farce for the book to be considered as essentially comic, and the features relating it to tragedy are surely as significant: the story of the Bundrens, like that of the Compsons or the Sutpens, is the story of a family adrift, with all its tensions and conflicts; it begins with the account of a last agony, ends with scenes of hatred, violence, and madness, and the two most remarkable characters in the novel—Addie and Darl—are both, because of their tortured awareness of their destiny, purely tragic figures. Lastly, *As I Lay Dying* also has unmistakable affinities with the epic: the terrible ordeals undergone by the Bundrens in the course of their journey and their valiant struggle against the unbridled elements inevitably bring to mind the heroic exploits of myth and legend. And the very idea which, according to Faulkner, gave rise to the novel appears, in its sheer simplicity, as an epic idea: "I took this family and subjected them to the two greatest catastrophies which man can suffer—flood and fire, that's all."[5]

Epic, tragedy, comedy? This is obviously not the right question to ask. To force the novel into the genres of traditional poetics is to ignore the dissonances from which it derives its originality. The distinctive aesthetic quality of *As I Lay Dying* is precisely that it is not an epic or a tragedy or a comedy, but, as it were, a gamble on being all three at once. It would perhaps be more worthwhile, therefore, to try another approach and see the novel through its narrative. What Faulkner is telling is the story of a journey. Now the journey is one of the narrative archetypes: from Homer's *Odyssey*[6] to Joyce's, from the adventurous navigators of mythology and folklore to the restless wandering heroes of the modern novel and cinema, it has held its place through countless variations as one of the basic patterns of narration. On reading *As I Lay Dying,* one might almost think that the novelist sought to bring into play the different forms that travelers' tales have taken over the centuries, or at least to make echoes of them reverberate throughout. In the humble state of its protagonists, in the pithy vigor of its realism and the earthy tang of its humor, the novel—a story about people on the road —recalls the picaresque tradition (Anse would easily qualify for the role of the rogue). In the weirdness of its atmosphere and the often wildly implausible nature of the reported events, it makes one think of the marvelous or fantastic journeys of folktale, epic, and myth. Behind this polarity of the real and the imaginary, the distinction between "novel" and "romance" established by Simms and Hawthorne, and taken up by Richard Chase,[7] will be easily recognized. On the face of it, *As I Lay Dying* may be taken for a rustic novel, but it is primarily a "romance" in the great symbolist tradition of American literature. If only in the motif of the strenuous journey, with all its wealth of connotations, it continues the exploration and illustration of a theme which, from the novels of James Fenimore Cooper through *Moby Dick* and *Huckleberry Finn,* has been central to American fiction.

The baffling diversity of tones and moods which characterizes the novel goes some way towards explaining the variety of interpretations it has provoked. *As I Lay Dying* offers us at once a comedy and the reverse of comedy, a tragedy and the derision of tragedy, an epic and the parody of epic. Is this simply the wry dialectic of humor, or is it not rather that the ruling force is irony? By thus forcing different genres to swallow each other, does one not end by clearing the way for absurdity? Judging by the closing pages, one might indeed think that absurdity wins the day. When Darl bursts out laughing at the monkeylike spectacle of his banana-munching family, it is hard to tell on which side lies reason and on which side madness. And in the final scene—which rings like a mocking echo of the recognition scenes one finds in the sentimental novels of the eighteenth century— when Anse, "kind of hangdog and proud too" (p. 250), introduces the new, duck-shaped and pop-eyed Mrs. Bundren to his perplexed children, the whole novel seems to tumble into sheer grotesqueness. As for the journey itself, it may seem quite as preposterous as this farcical ending. The stubbornness of the Bundrens in pursuing their funeral task reminds one at times of the blind obstinacy of burying beetles, and the result of their undertaking is perhaps less a victory of willpower than the triumph of inertia.

Are we then to conclude that all the values traditionally associated with the perilous journey are here reversed for the purpose of travesty, and that the epic overtones of the tale are only intended to point up the utter incongruity of this funeral steeplechase? Or is the burlesque not aimed rather at masking the praise of that eminently Faulknerian virtue, endurance? That irony informs the whole design of *As I Lay Dying* is beyond dispute. The point is that it may be read in more than one way. There is little justification therefore in singling out one pattern of meaning and imposing it on the novel as the only valid interpretation. As a matter of fact, all attempts to date at explaining its metaphysics or codifying its ethics have been more or less arbitrary oversimplifications. As one critic very rightly notes: "The novel has a wonderful immunity to schematization; it is innocent of both a moral and a morality, and it seems to breathe out rather than posit a world view."[8]

Faulkner here describes a world both absurd and living. He does not tell us whether we should reject the living as absurd, or accept the absurd as living. *As I Lay Dying* leaves its readers in a state of enthralled perplexity very similar to the stupor of the novel's characters in the face of what happens to them. This is not to say that the book cannot be discussed. To be satisfied with a single meaning, however, would be to misunderstand the subtle interplay of its ambiguities.

When Faulkner was questioned on *As I Lay Dying,* he invariably replied that it was a *tour de force*.[9] As much by the speed with which it was written as by the audacity of its technique and the superb virtuosity of its art, the novel is precisely that. It charms like a brilliant impromptu, dazzles like a perfectly executed trapeze exercise. Of all Faulkner's novels, it is perhaps the most agile, the most adroit, the one in which the writer's mastery of his craft and the versatility of his gifts reveal themselves in the most spectacular way. It is also, beneath its guise of an improvisation, one of his most complex and most intriguing works. Faulkner no doubt wrote more ambitious and more deeply moving books: *As I Lay Dying* does not achieve the grandeur of *The Sound and the Fury,* the novelist's most "splendid failure";[10] it does not hold us under the same dark spell as *Absalom, Absalom!* nor does it offer the imaginative scope of *Go Down, Moses.* But only slightly below these peaks, it holds its place as a masterpiece.[11]

2

Genesis and Sources

GENESIS

In OCTOBER 1929, when he began *As I Lay Dying,* Faulkner was just thirty-two. Besides texts which had appeared in periodicals, his published work already comprised five books: a collection of poems (*The Marble Faun*) and four novels (*Soldiers' Pay, Mosquitoes, Sartoris, The Sound and the Fury*). Although the young novelist was not entirely unknown and had begun, especially since the publication of *The Sound and the Fury* (October 7, 1929), to enjoy a measure of renown in literary circles, none of his books had sold well. To earn a living Faulkner was reduced to accepting all sorts of odd jobs. Married since the summer of 1929 to Estelle Oldham, he had just settled with his wife in a modest apartment in Oxford, Mississippi. At night he worked as a stoker in the power plant of the University of Mississippi, and it was there during the long nights that he wrote *As I Lay Dying,* in circumstances he described some years later in his preface to the Modern Library edition of *Sanctuary:*

> I got a job in the power plant, on the night shift, from 6 P.M. to 6 A.M., as a coal passer. I shoveled coal from the bunker into a wheel-barrow and wheeled it in and dumped it where the fireman could put it into the boiler. About 11 o'clock the people would be going to bed, and so it did not take so much steam. Then we could

rest, the fireman and I. He would sit in a chair and doze. I had invented a table out of a wheel-barrow in the coal bunker, just beyond
a wall from where a dynamo ran. It made a deep, constant hum-
ming noise. There was no more work to do until about 4 A.M.,
when we would have to clean the fires and get up steam again. On
these nights, between 12 and 4, I wrote *As I Lay Dying* in six weeks,
without changing a word. I sent it to Smith and wrote him that by
it I would stand or fall.[1]

What needs to be remembered here, apart from the remarkable circumstances of the composition of the novel, is the statement, repeated by the author in several subsequent interviews,[2]
that *As I Lay Dying* was written in the space of six weeks without
the slightest alteration. Should this statement be accepted literally? There is no doubt that the novel was written with unusual
swiftness: the first page of the manuscript is dated "25 october
1929," the last "Oxford, Miss./11 December, 1929." As for the
typescript, it was done by January 12, 1930, a date likewise noted
by Faulkner.[3] If one accepts the indications given in the manuscript, the composition of the novel did in fact take little more
than six weeks. Yet to these six weeks one needs to add the month
Faulkner took to type his manuscript: a comparison of the two
texts provides substantial evidence that the typing up involved a
process of meticulous revision.

It matters little whether the novel was written in six or ten
weeks. But Faulkner was obviously not quite telling the truth
when he claimed to have changed nothing of his first draft. The
manuscript itself shows clearly that the book is nothing less than
the result of hasty improvisation. It is true that certain pages give
the impression of having found their final form from the very
outset. Most of them, however, bear the traces of numerous corrections. Thus on the first page of the manuscript, which corresponds to the first section of the published book, there are sixteen
deletions, with more than fifty words crossed out, and a short
sentence appears in the margin, with a line indicating where it
should be inserted in the text.[4] Almost the whole of the manu-

script shows modifications of this order: deletions, additions, and substitutions relating to words, sentences, or parts of sentences, more rarely to whole paragraphs. As in most of Faulkner's manuscripts, a wide margin is allowed at the left of each sheet so that additions can be made without overloading the text with emendations. Often these marginal notations are of a descriptive character, aimed either at heightening the relief of certain scenes or at rounding off the portrayal of some character. For example, in the second section, Cora Tull's description of Addie's dying is completed by the following details: "The quilt is drawn up to her chin, hot as it is, with only her two hands and her face outside" (holograph, p. 2; published version, p. 8). Similarly, when Faulkner recounts the Tulls' return from the funeral service, he begins by noting that Cora continues singing hymns, then adds in the margin: "sitting on the wagon seat, the shawl around her shoulders and the umbrella open above her head" (holograph, p. 36; slightly different published version, p. 86). Elsewhere there are additions to the dialogue, like Anse's satisfied reflection that Cash was lucky to have broken the same leg twice (holograph, p. 75; published version, p. 176), or the brief conversation between Armstid and his outraged wife about the stinking corpse (holograph, p. 76; published version, p. 178). Like a painter, Faulkner adds stroke after stroke to build up a total picture with "form solidity colour."[5] His sureness of touch rarely fails him: nothing is overdone; far from interrupting the first flow of invention or deflecting its course, each marginal note fits quite naturally into the general movement of Faulkner's prose and enriches its texture without ever marring it.

On examining the typescript (which is almost identical with the printed version), one soon realizes that this process of expansion and revision continued after the manuscript was completed. Such modifications as are made hardly affect the structure of the novel. The order of the sections remains unchanged except for one very short Cash section (p. 157: "It wasn't on a balance . . . ") which for reasons of credibility is shifted from thirty-sixth to thirty-eighth place. Nor is there any new element in the story except the brief incident on the outskirts of Jefferson between Jewel and the man who commented on the smell from Addie's coffin (pp. 219–20), an episode which had only been alluded to in the manuscript. Many sections, it is true, have increased in length and some of them have been quite considerably reworked (notably sections 7 and 30, both monologues by the inarticulate Dewey Dell), but most of the corrections are concerned with details of expression. Thus at the end of the first section, as if afraid of being too explicit, the author substitutes "finished box" for "coffin" and "Addie Bundren" for "Maw" (p. 4) : the manuscript left no doubt as to the nature of the box and defined from the start the family relationship between Darl and Addie; the words used in the final version are more ambiguous, and we have to read on for the uncertainties to be resolved.[6] Other changes could readily be found which create ambiguity. One of them is the replacement of nouns by personal pronouns without immediate antecedents: in the manuscript, the buzzards hovering over the funeral cortège are specified by name at the end of section 25; in the published text, "buzzards" is replaced by "they," and the meaning of the sentence—"Behind us, above the house, motionless in tall and soaring circles, they diminish and disappear" (p. 98)—can be understood only through its echo of the first reference to the creatures in section 21: "Motionless, the tall buzzards hang in roaring circles . . ." (p. 89). Other alterations are intended to suggest more forcefully the immediacy of sensory perception: in the admirable description of Jewel and his horse in section 3, the image of the horse "glinting for a gaudy instant among the *pines*" (holograph, p. 4) becomes "glinting for a gaudy instant among the *blue shadows* (p. 11). From an objective observation one passes to a subjective impression, from a neutral reference to a vivid visual image. It is clear that if in revising this novel, Faulkner often sought sharper realism, he also had recourse to the power of poetic suggestion. His is an art, like that of Verlaine and the French Symbolists, whom he read in his youth, "in which Uncertain and Precise are wed."[7]

Finally, many stylistic changes bear witness to the care with which Faulkner individualized the language of each character and to his subtlety in using diction and syntax as a means of characterization. In the second version of Whitfield's monologue (pp. 169–71), for instance, he substitutes stately Latinisms with strong biblical connotations for the plain words he had used in his first draft ("I emerged victorious" for "I won," "repair" for "go," "perish" for "die," "eternity" for "death"), adds sonorous phrases like the "awful and irrevocable judgment," multiplies allusions to Christ ("the scene of my Gethsemane"), and thus ironically emphasizes the sanctimonious solemnity of the preacher's rhetoric.[8]

There can be no question here of analyzing all the textual variants. But the examples given above will serve to indicate the scrupulous attention with which Faulkner undertook the revision of this novel. It is true that the corrections, although numerous, are almost all minor. Everything suggests that when he began to write *As I Lay Dying,* the novelist was already in full possession of all the data and knew what form he would give his book. If the manuscript betrays some hesitation on secondary points (people's names, use of italics, of tenses, etc.), the plan of the novel is already fixed, and there is no trace of doubt over the method of narrative management or the handling of viewpoints. The fictional technique, despite its originality, is not the result of long and patient efforts; it appears to have imposed itself of its own accord, to have arisen from the vision— what Faulkner calls his "dream"—as part and parcel of it:

> Sometimes technique charges in and takes command of the dream before the writer himself can get his hands on it. That is *tour de force* and the finished work is simply a matter of fitting bricks

neatly together, since the writer knows probably every single word right to the end before he puts the first one down. This happened with *As I Lay Dying*. It was not easy. No honest work is. It was simple in that all the material was already at hand.[9]

Other novels by Faulkner—among them the greatest—went through a more difficult gestation period. *As I Lay Dying* was not the struggle with the Angel that *The Sound and the Fury* had been: Faulkner was doubtless never to know again the agony and the "ecstasy"[10] he had experienced when trying to tell the tragic story of Caddy Compson. Here the relationship which developed between the writer and his work seems to have been less emotional, more relaxed, easier to control. Giving up the idea of a second struggle with the impossible, he approached his creation with greater detachment and perfect ease. Everything here seems given, sprung from a marvelously alert invention and at the same time controlled at every turn by a novelist in full command of his craft. *As I Lay Dying* offers us perhaps the most dazzling performance of Faulkner's creative exuberance; it also reveals the exemplary probity and vigilance of an artist who had learned to mistrust the facile and whose every work is haunted by the stringent and never satisfied demands of perfection.

SOURCES

They are people that I have known all my life in the country I was born in. The actions, the separate actions, I may have seen, remembered. It was the imagination probably that tied the whole thing together into a story. It's difficult to say just what part of any story comes specifically from imagination, what part from experience, what part from observation. It's like having . . . three tanks with a collector valve. And you don't know just how much comes from which tank. All you know is a stream of water runs from the valve when you open it, drawn from the three tanks—observation, experience, imagination.[11]

That was Faulkner's reply to a West Point cadet who had asked him somewhat naively where he "got the idea" for *As I*

Lay Dying. It tells us nothing precise about the sources of the novel, except that there is nothing precise to tell. From things seen, anecdotes heard, impressions recorded day by day in a memory always ready and willing, from such scattered fragments was the novel constructed. As for the locale of the book, it was the land where Faulkner was born and reared, the region of northern Mississippi where he was to spend most of his life. Like all the novels of the Yoknapatawpha cycle, *As I Lay Dying* is firmly rooted in this "little postage stamp of native soil"[12] whose inexhaustible fertility Faulkner had just discovered and on which he intended to draw for the material of his personal "cosmos."

As I Lay Dying was Faulkner's third novel to deal with Yoknapatawpha County and its people. Unlike *Sartoris* and *The Sound and the Fury,* however, it introduces us to an exclusively rural world, and among the author's early works its only predecessor in this respect is "The Liar," a short story published in 1925.[13] On Faulkner's map it is located in the Frenchman's Bend area, southeast of Jefferson. In social terms the novel represents the writer's first serious incursion into the class of the poor whites of the Mississippi hill country. It probably was for him a less familiar world than that of the Sartorises and the Compsons, which he had explored in his two previous novels, and he may have found it easier therefore to maintain the detachment needed for humor. As for the incidents and characters of the book, it is of little interest to know whether they have their counterparts in real life. According to John B. Cullen, a citizen of Oxford and hunting companion of Faulkner's, the novelist may have remembered a family of shiftless farmers whose eccentricities had been a source of local gossip.[14] But the hypothesis is based on flimsy evidence, and in any event there is no question of there being a single model. The protagonists of *As I Lay Dying* are in no way characters from a *roman à clef*. It would likewise be incorrect to take them primarily as social

types. Faulkner managed to stay faithful to the genuine attitudes, gestures, and words of their everyday lives: in this sense
the Bundrens, Tulls, Armstids, and Samsons are indeed lifelike
Mississippi farmers. But by uprooting them from their native
soil and recasting them in the mold of his own imaginary world,
he made them inhabitants of that other South whose reality
exists only in fiction.

The primary source of *As I Lay Dying,* the most obvious and
the most elusive, is none other than the South itself. There is
nothing surprising in that when one knows that almost all
Faulkner's books share the same source. As far as literary sources
are concerned, they are certainly just as tricky to determine with
any precision. The technical debt to Joyce is apparent, but as in
The Sound and the Fury, Faulkner uses the Joycean "stream-of-
consciousness" method to his own ends, not hesitating to depart
from his model whenever it suits his purposes.[15] Another influence is that of T. S. Eliot: already perceptible in his early poems,
it may also be traced in most of the novels Faulkner wrote in
the 20s and 30s, and is almost embarrassingly conspicuous in
Pylon (1935). In *As I Lay Dying,* as in *The Sound and the
Fury,* it remains unobtrusive. But there is an unmistakable family likeness between Faulkner's novel and *The Waste Land,*
published in 1922: the same obsession with death in its two
forms of physical decay and spiritual aridity (one of the sections of the poem is entitled "The Burial of the Dead"), the
same atmosphere of cosmic desolation and exhaustion (the expression "the dead land" appears both in Eliot and Faulkner),
the use of the same elemental imagery and symbolism (fire and
water), parallel references to myth and ritual. To these similarities of a thematic or symbolic order one might add some surprising ones of detail: thus two of the most significant objects
in the novel—the false teeth and the gramophone—are already
mentioned in the poem. It would be wrong however to attach
too much importance to these analogies. Most of them are either

too general or too tenuous to be accredited with any certainty to Eliot's influence.[16] It seems even more dubious to consider Sir James Frazer's *Golden Bough* as a major source of the novel.[17] It is now an established fact that Faulkner had read Frazer's book during his stay with Sherwood Anderson in New Orleans,[18] and it is safe to assume that his work profited from it. But in none of his novels, with the exception of *A Fable,* does one find a methodical transposition of an existing mythical model, and one would search in vain for such an elaborate network of correspondences as links Joyce's *Ulysses* to Homer's *Odyssey. As I Lay Dying* incorporates mythical reminiscences from various sources. Some stem from local folklore, others from biblical and Christian tradition;[19] still others seem to take us back to the most archaic strata of the primitive mind. They all contribute towards a ritualization of the novel, expand the meaning of its symbols, and point its ironies. But to impose a ready-made pattern from some catalogued myth on the book would be to misunderstand completely the mechanism of Faulkner's creative method.

That Joyce, T. S. Eliot, and Frazer exercised a lasting influence on Faulkner could be established from novels other than *As I Lay Dying.* Are there any literary sources peculiar to this work? Several critics have been struck by the resemblances between *As I Lay Dying* and Hawthorne's masterpiece, *The Scarlet Letter.*[20] These resemblances are hardly apparent in the narrative structure, but between the two central figures—Addie Bundren and Hester Prynne—the parallel is indeed striking. Passionate, imperious women, proudly ensconced in their solitude, they are also both unfaithful wives. Disappointed by their husbands (whose inadequacy is underscored in both novels by a slight deformity), they throw themselves into adultery out of scorn and defiance, and both choose a minister as a lover, as if by adding sacrilege to lust they wanted to place their sin beyond atonement. Whitfield and Dimmesdale (whose very names are formed in a similar way: white, dim; field, dale) are also related figures: men of God reputed for their piety, sinners tormented in secret by remorse, they are weak-minded hypocrites, unworthy of their partners. But whereas Dimmesdale ends by freeing himself from his sense of guilt through a public confession which costs him his life, Whitfield remains to the end a prisoner of his moral cowardice and bad faith.[21] Worthy of note also is the vital role played in the two novels by the children born of the illicit liaison. Like Hester, Addie is violently attached to her illegitimate child (and here again the symbolism of the names —Pearl and Jewel—accentuates the resemblance between the characters), who is instrumental in her salvation. But if Pearl rescues her mother from despair, Jewel saves a mere corpse. In fact it will be seen that the differences are as significant as the similarities: Whitfield is at best a grotesque version of Dimmesdale; Pearl's eerie grace and sensitivity are poles apart from Jewel's brutal passion, Chillingworth's icy and morose intellectuality from Anse's whining craftiness; and while Hawthorne depicts Hester's moral trials, Faulkner devotes three-quarters of his tale to the tribulations of Addie's rotting corpse. It looks almost as if *As I Lay Dying* were conceived as a subtle and sinister parody of *The Scarlet Letter*. Was the parallel intentionally pursued or is it simply the result of a chance encounter? Questioned on that point in 1957, Faulkner replied:

No, a writer don't have to consciously parallel because he robs and steals from everything he ever wrote or read or saw. I was simply writing a *tour de force* and as every writer does, I took whatever I needed wherever I could find it, without any compunction and with no sense of violating any ethics or hurting anyone's feeling because any writer feels that anyone after him is perfectly welcome to take any trick he has learned or any plot he has used. Of course we don't know just who Hawthorne took his from. Which he probably did because there are so few plots to write about.[22]

While Faulkner denies taking Hawthorne as a model, he defends every novelist's right to borrow from any quarter the materials and tools he needs to construct his work. It is a prerogative he exercised unashamedly, as Dickens, Balzac, and Joyce had before him. But as the last sentence of the above quotation suggests, this freedom to borrow and steal as by right is the obverse of a restraint from which no novelist can escape: that of drawing the elements of his work from a common fund. He is consequently never entirely free to invent his plot; the number of narrative structures is limited, and they have all been used before. The same could be said of the other elements in his work. The stock from which they are drawn is a *finite* one. As Claude Lévi-Strauss has demonstrated, the creation of myths works within similar boundaries:

> The characteristic feature of mythical thought is that it expresses itself by means of a heterogeneous repertoire which even if extensive, is nevertheless limited. It has to use this repertoire, however, whatever the task in hand because it has nothing else at its disposal. Mythical thought is therefore a kind of intellectual bricolage— which explains the relation which can be perceived between the two.[23]

What makes Faulkner the heir and perpetuator of this type of thought and assures him a place among the great mythopoeic novelists is not the occasional reference to mythological figures found in his books, or even the parallels to mythical patterns discernible there, but precisely the way in which—from the heterogeneous variety of sources to the organic unity of the finished novel—his creative work is accomplished. Neither invention *ex nihilo* nor servile submission to earlier models, Faulkner's creation goes in search of its own structures through a careful and complex reordering of all the debris and residues it finds on its way. One does not diminish his achievement by calling it inspired "bricolage."

3

Language and Style

The Sound and the Fury and *As I Lay Dying* marked Faulkner's almost miraculous leap to artistic maturity. In these two novels his style achieved for the first time complete mastery of its powers, leaving the naive gropings and self-conscious sophistication of his earlier works far behind. No trace is left in them of the florid descriptions and prolix dialogues which marred *Soldiers' Pay* and *Mosquitoes,* nor is there anything to remind us of the lushness and looseness one occasionally still finds in *Sartoris.* At this point in his career, the resources of language no longer held any secrets for Faulkner, and he now exploited them with an assurance, an exactness, and a dexterity verging on virtuosity.

As I Lay Dying offers a brilliant demonstration of this brio: the superb ease with which the novelist moves from one narrator to another and modulates their voices almost calls to mind a stylistic exercise. At one end of the gamut is the simple, brisk, and racy idiom of the Mississippi farmers; at the other, the pyrotechnics of Darl's rhetoric. But this preliminary distinction only indicates the width of Faulkner's range; it does not begin to suggest the countless variations and nuances found in his prose. His style explores so many possibilities, uses so many devices, changes tone, timbre, or tempo so often that it may seem pointless to look for a unifying principle. Faulkner's medium is in fact a combination of several styles. But how can these styles be sorted out?

One might try a classification by function, distinguishing between the straightforward, colloquial style of the dialogues, the precise and rapid style of narration, and the richly suggestive style of the descriptions. Such a classification, however, could not fail to raise objections, for the distance between the three styles varies considerably according to the identity of the speaker. The stylistic difference between a reported conversation and a fragment of narrative is almost nil in the case of Tull (who narrates as he talks) while it is very marked with Darl (who narrates as Faulkner writes). For the same reason, no clear line can be drawn between narrative and descriptive style. There is certainly a narrative style common to Tull, Samson, and Armstid, but in the Darl sections it is impossible to dissociate narrative from description. What makes it so difficult to categorize style according to function is the fact that the mode of expression is almost always determined by character. In *As I Lay Dying* every character speaks in his own voice, and the reader is soon able to distinguish between Darl's taut, dense, metaphorical style, Anse's placid sententiousness, Cora's cant and cackle, and Vardaman's helpless stutterings. Faulkner has orchestrated all these voices with admirable skill and effectiveness, sometimes counterpointing them, playing them off against one another to emphasize contrasts (putting Addie's monologue, for instance, between Cora's and Whitfield's), sometimes using their resemblances to point out affinities which bind one character to another (as Cora to Whitfield in the above example). This chameleonic, plural style gives the measure of Faulkner's prodigious gifts for verbal mimicry. Yet, sharply individualized as they are, the characters' voices seldom possess the objective status of dramatic representation; they do not prevent us from hearing the author's voice throughout the novel.

3 · LANGUAGE AND STYLE

DICTION

FAULKNER's presence makes itself felt first of all through the wealth and variety of his diction. The basic vocabulary is that of common speech, specifically the dialect spoken by the small hill farmers in northeastern Mississippi; it is the rough and simple vocabulary of uneducated country people, bristling with improprieties and deformations.

These deformations stem partly from the peculiarities of Southern pronunciation, which Faulkner made a point of transcribing: *hit* for *it* (*passim*), *ere* for *here* (*passim;* note that *ere* is used as a demonstrative and sometimes takes the sense of *any*), *ketch* for *catch* (p. 41), *kin* for *can* (p. 42), *keer* for *care* (p. 43), *jest* for *just* (p. 43), *gal* for *girl* (pp. 119, 130, 133, 179), *sho* for *sure* (pp. 174, 179, 180), *dust* for *dusk* (pp. 69, 105), *mast* for *mask* (p. 69), etc. It should be noted however that phonetic transcription is used by Faulkner with remarkable restraint: in the manuscript *hit* occurs far more often than in the final version, and it seems as though the author refused to rely too heavily on the rather facile effect of such transcriptions. (Strangely enough, they are nowhere as numerous as in the conversations reported in section 11 by Doctor Peabody, who apparently enjoys aping the speech of his boorish patients).

To these pronunciation features must be added most of the morphological and grammatical deviations prevalent in substandard American English. As far as verbs are concerned, one finds, apart from the usual contraction *aint*:

The auxiliary *was* used in the plural: *we was across* (p. 131); *they was in the kitchen* (p. 68); *they was setting in the wagon* (p. 117).
The third person singular inflection extended to other persons: *I says* (p. 35); *you fixes it* (p. 99); *his folks buries* (p. 28).
Weak preterites used for strong verbs (*knowed, passim; throwed,* p. 37; *growed,* p. 37; *blowed,* p. 41) and, more rarely,

strong preterites used for weak verbs (the old form *holp* for *helped*, pp. 32, 85).

Past participles used as preterites (*you seen it*, p. 67; *I taken the mule*, p. 117) and preterites used as participles (*he might have fell*, p. 178).

Double suffixes for weak verbs (*drownded* instead of *drowned*, pp. 66, 67).

Present participles preceded by *a-* (*a-laying*, p. 34; *a-moving*, pp. 34–35, and *passim*), archaic forms often used by Faulkner for rhythmic effect.

Pronoun forms and inflection patterns are also frequently in contradiction with accepted norms:

The inflection of *mine* and *thine* extended by analogy to the possessive pronouns for the third person singular (*hisn*, p. 85; *hern*, p. 86) and the first person plural (*ourn*, pp. 87, 120).

Hisself substituted for the reflexive pronoun *himself* (p. 31). Objective forms of personal pronouns substituted for the subject (*me and him were born close together*, p. 224) and *them* used as a demonstrative (*one of them spotted shoats*, p. 148).

The list of these deviant forms could easily be lengthened. They are instrumental in establishing the social and cultural level of the characters, but would be inadequate on their own to give their language its distinctive rustic and regional flavor. This is created principally by the use of certain turns of phrase like *It's fixing to rain* (see sections 5, 8, and 9); rural colloquialisms like *tyke* (pp. 32, 33, 43), *critter* (pp. 65, 98), and *cattymount* (p. 98); archaisms like *beholden* (pp. 110, 111) or the saying *quick with young* (p. 72); and "Southernisms" such as *peakling* (p. 17) and *pussel-gutted* (pp. 13, 39).[1]

This rustic vocabulary serves essentially to designate the concrete and familiar world of everyday life. But whenever these country people experience the need to express ideas or feelings, we see them turn naturally to the Bible. In *As I Lay Dying*, the

biblical tradition, with all that Southern fundamentalist religion
in such a rural community adds in the way of violent emotional-
ism, shows through time and time again. Anse's and Tull's monologues, and even more Cora's and Whitfield's, are full of
religious references, and God is more than once invoked. As in
the Scriptures, the pronoun and possessives attached to the Lord
are given capitals; Anse, when he speaks of Him, comically
makes a point of adding the suffix -*eth* to all his verbs: "I am the
chosen of the Lord, for who He loveth, so doeth He chastiseth"
(p. 105). Anse's and his neighbors' God is the jealous God (cf.
p. 160) of the Old Testament, a God of wrath and vengeance,
distant, mysterious, and yet strangely humanized: it is as natural
to mention the hand of the Lord (p. 68) as the thigh of Satan
(p. 170). For all these Baptists and Methodists, the God of the
Bible and all the mythological and ideological background of
Christianity are an indispensable framework of reference, and
they have recourse to it whenever they attempt to translate their
experience of life into consciousness and give it a meaning. Thus
Addie describes herself as a sinner (her diction, though, seems
to refer at the same time to some primitive blood-and-earth religion beyond Christianity). For Anse (pp. 34–35) and Tull
(p. 68) the definition of wisdom comes down to a justification
of the ways of Providence, and God is called as a witness to the
world's misery: "If it's a judgment," cries Tull, almost rebel-
ling, "it aint right" (p. 70).

One should not however conclude, as have some overzealous
critics for whom everything is Christ to the mill, that *As I Lay
Dying* is a Christian novel. For these farmers—as, indeed, for
the novelist himself—this vocabulary is first and foremost a
tool. It may also be used as a screen: one of the many ironies
of the book is that for several of its characters these religious
references are purely verbal. Those who use them most readily
—Anse, Cora, Whitfield—are also the most hypocritical, and in
their devout speeches there is something that sounds not only

comic but also shallow and false. With Cora and Whitfield, for example, the words go in biblical pairs so often that their professions of faith have a mechanical ring: *the eternal and everlasting salvation and grace* (p. 8), *trials and tribulations* (p. 159), *sin and salvation* (p. 159), *danger and difficulties* (p. 169). One recalls Addie's diatribe against words: these repetitious, alliterative formulae are indeed nothing but deceitful and garrulous cant.

The characteristics we have noted so far—nearness to the spoken word, reliance on the plain diction of common speech, occasional use of biblical phrases—can all be related to the tradition of the vernacular narrative initiated in American literature by the humorists of the old Southwest and by Mark Twain. That Faulkner's prose is indebted to this tradition, no one will dispute. Yet the lexical resources it draws upon are by no means limited to the fund of colloquial speech. At the risk of forfeiting credibility, the novelist does not hesitate to endow at least some of his uncouth farmers with a richer and more refined vocabulary whenever it suits his purposes. In *As I Lay Dying* scarcely any of the minor characters are granted this privilege, with the plausible exception of Dr. Peabody. But young Vardaman, who hardly knows how to talk, suddenly comes out with abstract terms like *integrity, unrelated, components,* and *coordinated* (p. 55). As for Darl, not only does he express himself with amazing correctness (except when telling the story of Jewel and his horse in section 32) but his vocabulary is also infinitely more varied and more learned than that of those around him. Here is a sample:

pantomime (p. 47), *sibilance* (p. 48), *penurious* (p. 50), *ubiquity* (p. 51), *silhouette* (pp. 72, 75), *elongation* (p. 72), *reverberant* (p. 72), *precautionary* (p. 75), *retrograde* (pp. 89, 216), *volitional* (p. 91), *emaciation* (p. 92), *capitulation* (p. 102), *scoriation* (p. 102), *circumscribed* (p. 135), *accretion*

(p. 139), *cubistic* (p. 209), *proscenium* (p. 211), *reaccruent* (p. 216).

In these sonorous polysyllables any Faulkner reader will recognize the author's penchant for Latinisms. With Darl, we enter the specifically Faulknerian lexical domain, and it is also in his monologues that the peculiarities of its implementation are most clearly perceptible. Many of the author's favorites are to be found there, most of them being key words in his thematic developments: philosophical concepts such as *time, space, motion;* moral and psychological abstractions like *astonishment, fear, outrage, terror, fury, pride, despair;* and, throughout the novel, epithets such as *profound, terrible, terrific, motionless, alert, sad, wild, calm, composed.* Far from being superadded, these words are always woven into the concrete texture of the novel. The close conjunction between physical particulars and abstractions is one of the most typical features of Faulkner's style. The effect of combining them often grips us by its strangeness: "And Cash like sawing the long hot sad yellow days up into planks and nailing them to something" (p. 25). A similar effect is obtained by the rhetorical device of hypallage, i.e., the transfer of concrete epithets to abstract nouns: *his slack-faced astonishment* (p. 72), *awry-feathered, disgruntled outrage* (p. 48), *a curled, gnarled inertness* (p. 50). These singular combinations bring about a sort of reciprocal contamination of the terms juxtaposed: the abstract, weighed down with materiality, solidifies and acquires the quality of immediate presence while the concrete loses substance and tends to evaporate into the universal.

Another aspect of Faulkner's diction is the profusion of words with a negating prefix or suffix. These "negative ultimates," as one critic has called them,[2] express in turn:

The inability to understand or believe: *meaningless* (p. 209), *unbelief* (p. 208), *unbelievably* (p. 212).

Fixity: *motionless* (*passim*), an index to Faulkner's concern with stasis and motion.
The idea of fatality: *irrevocable* (pp. 46, 171), *irremediable* (p. 46).
The ephemeral and immaterial: *impermanent* (p. 134), *invisible* (pp. 71, 92), *impalpable* (p. 72), *voiceless* (p. 167) and *voicelessness* (p. 166), *soundless* (p. 208), *lifeless* (p. 75). The lack of ending: *endless* (p. 209), *interminable* (p. 209).

Like Milton and Melville, Faulkner felt the need to add to these terms some negatives of his own coinage: *unalone* (p. 59), *unlamped* (p. 76), *uninferant* (p. 101), *unvirgin* (p. 165), *unwinded* (pp. 134, 216). Even more striking are all the negatives created by the addition of *no* or *not* as a suffix (*is-not*, p. 76) and more especially as a prefix: *not-fish* (p. 52), *not-blood* (p. 52), *not-moving* (p. 185), *not-Anse* (p. 166), and in a single one of Darl's sentences *no-wind, no-sound, no-hand, no-strings* (p. 196). All these negatives refer us back to the theme of absence, of lack, of nothingness which, as we shall see, pervades the whole novel; they are also indicative of Faulkner's obstinate efforts to overcome the inadequacy of language: they attempt to express the inexpressible. It should be noted too that they are not simply the reverse of an affirmation: the negation preserves within the substance of the word the idea of what it is denying and paradoxically it sometimes even reinforces the meaning it might be supposed to deny. Thus *unalone* (p. 59) epitomizes admirably what pregnancy is making Dewey Dell go through: a solitude both violated and redoubled.

Faulkner was at pains to restore to language all its powers of suggestion. Hence, in his novels, the search for the most compact form, which often makes him condense his discourse to the point of opacity. Hence, too, his verbal inventiveness designed to correct the shortcomings and offset the diffuseness of ordinary speech, which manifests itself most notably in the creation of compounds. In *As I Lay Dying* these are fewer, less unusual, and less evocative than in *Light in August* or *Pylon*. Some of them, however, are surprising enough: *crop-toothed* (p. 12; turned around as *tooth-cropped* on page 174), *grease-fouled* (p. 71), *bone-gaunted* (p. 108), *spraddle-legged* (p. 112), *dangle-armed* (pp. 51, 181).

If compounds play no prominent part in *As I Lay Dying*, the novel illustrates abundantly Faulkner's taste for accumulation, particularly with respect to adjectives. Epithets indeed seldom come singly, and often there are clusters of three, four, or even five attached to a single noun:

the long hot sad yellow days [p. 25]
an expression sudden, intent, and concerned [p. 97]
a wild, sad, profound and despairing quality [p. 139]
his pale empty sad composed and questioning face [p. 115]

This piling up of qualifying words is intended to achieve through cumulative effect what the effort of concision attempts to collect and retain in the energy of a single word. But whether Faulkner coins new words or hurls them in handfuls onto the page, the driving force is still the same rage for expression, the same compulsive need to say everything.[3]

SYNTAX

THE curious combination of a rough-edged spoken language and an ostensibly literary language that may be detected in the diction of *As I Lay Dying* is present as well in its syntax. Faulkner was not content to sprinkle a few regionalisms over his prose, to put a few touches of local color here and there for the mere pleasure of being picturesque. The relationship between the spoken and the written word is both closer and more subtle: in fact, it is to the creative interplay between the colloquial and the literary tradition that Faulkner's style owes its rugged vigor and vitality. His prose, however controlled in its effects, is almost always attuned to the pulse of living speech. In some of his books, to be sure, the vocal comes close to the oratorical, the stream of words broadens and swells into torrential rhetoric. Nothing like this happens in *As I Lay Dying:* it does not contain any of those endless, involuted, labyrinthine sentences in which the reader sometimes gets lost in *Absalom, Absalom!* or *Go Down, Moses.* The syntax of the novel is often modeled on the patterns of oral communication; it may become loose and verge on obscurity when the novelist tries to recreate the discontinuity and incoherence of psychical processes, but it never becomes so dislocated as to be unintelligible.

Grammar, it is true, is often roughly handled. To the oddities already listed, another one might be added here, namely double, even triple, negation:

> I reckon she *never* had *no* use for them now. [p. 7]
> But I just *cant* seem to get *no* heart into it. [p. 37]
> He *couldn't* buy *no* team from *nobody*. [p. 179]

These double negatives underline the generally pleonastic and redundant character of spoken language. With the exception of Darl and Addie (in their monologues reiteration also occurs, but in another way), the characters' speeches all abound in repetitions. The same words and phrases recur time and time again; countless sentences are produced from identical molds, as is evidenced by the frequency of the verb *to aim,* which is almost used as an auxiliary, and the many sentences beginning with *I reckon* or punctuated by *durn*. Yet for Faulkner it is not merely a matter of transcribing verbal tics. Repetition serves other purposes. It multiplies echoes and thus contributes to underpinning and unifying the thematic structure of the novel; it may also function as a device of characterization: this is the case with Jewel's *goddamn,* Cash's *It wont balance,* and all Anse's clichés, which could be compared to characters' set phrases in the theater, and equivalents of which would be easy to find in earlier novelists, like Balzac or Dickens. Through repetition, through words and sentences ricocheting from one paragraph to another, from one section to another, the characters' idiosyncrasies are revealed and their secret obsessions betrayed in all their comic or pathetic urgency: Dewey Dell's monologue in section 14 includes five slightly modified repetitions of the opening sentence, "He could do so much for me . . ." (cf. pp. 56–61), and throughout the novel Vardaman recites such incantatory formulae as "My mother is a fish" or "Darl is my brother."

Repetition, then, is never used at random. Much the same could be said of the syntax of the book, a syntax distinguished neither by the orthodoxy of its grammar nor by the rigor of its logic, but admirably suited to render the immediate impact and fullness of sensory perception as well as the ripples and eddies of emotional experience.

At the simplest level one finds here, as in Mark Twain, Sherwood Anderson or Hemingway, strings of simple declarative sentences, sometimes juxtaposed:

The signboard passes; the unscarred road wheels on. Then Dewey Dell turns her head. The wagon creaks on. [p. 102]

sometimes joined by *and:*

So Jewel got the team and come for me and they fixed me a pallet in the wagon and we drove across the square where pa said, and we was waiting there in the wagon. . . . [p. 249]

But the order of words and the coordination of clauses by no means always conform to this rudimentary pattern. The monotony of this paratactic style—very marked in the Vardaman sections—is frequently broken by the use of constructional devices which here have nothing "literary" about them, since they are the very same as those one encounters in the spontaneous eloquence of everyday speech. One of them is inversion:

A good carpenter, Cash is [p. 4]
New Hope, 3 mi. it will say [p. 114]
Kind of pleased astonishment he looked [p. 117]

Many elliptical constructions are also to be found. Either part of the statement is missing ("Glad to go," p. 22), or a clause of the sentence is omitted ("Which is a good thing," p. 68; "Because Jewel is too hard on him," p. 223), or the sentence is uncompleted, like those which end two of Cash's monologues (cf. pp. 90, 157). The sentences beginning with "It's because" might be considered part of this type of construction:

It's because he stays out there, right under the window, hammering and sawing on that goddamn box. [p. 14]
It's because I am alone [p. 56]

Although grammatically correct, these sentences do not fulfill their promises. *It's* in no way defines what the causal subordinate clause appears to explain. In fact, it is only pseudocausal, indicating not the apprehension of a cause-and-effect relationship but a total failure to understand.[4]

Naturally enough, the most peculiar sentence structures occur in those parts of the monologues where linguistic coherence tends to melt into the "stream of consciousness." Mental disarray makes itself felt through the suppression of semantic links or by irregularities and breaks in construction. In a sentence of Vardaman's like "Pa shaves every day now because my mother is a fish" (p. 95), syntactic coordination is normal, but objectively speaking the statement of the subordinate clause as well as the causal relation between the two clauses are absurd. The grammatical connection itself disappears in this anacoluthon of Dewey Dell's: "It's because in the wild and outraged earth too soon too soon too soon" (p. 114). The meaning of this sentence, however, is not entirely incongruous, it is simply obscured by the distortion of the syntax.

The unsettling effect can also stem from the substitution of one grammatical category for another (grammatical metaphor). *As I Lay Dying* provides several examples of substantivized verbal forms, particularly in Darl's puzzling play on the verb *to be:*

> And since sleep is is-not and rain and wind are *was,* it is not. Yet the wagon *is,* because when the wagon is *was,* Addie Bundren will not be. And Jewel is, so Addie Bundren must be. And then I must be, or I could not empty myself for sleep in a strange room. And so if am not emptied yet, I am *is.* [p. 76]

In Darl, this misapplication of grammatical categories underscores the difficulty of positing identity (noun) in time and motion (verb). In Vardaman, it proceeds not from metaphysical perplexities, but from a child's bewilderment in a moment of emotional stress, as can be seen in the following statement, where the confusion between the literal and metaphorical meanings of *to go* (to go to Jackson, to go crazy) induces the absurd equation of *crazy* with the place name:

> My brother he went crazy and he went to Jackson too. Jackson is further away than crazy. [p. 242]

Even more disturbing in its effects, the suppression of punctuation not only breaks up syntactic relationships but tends to annul them. In Dewey Dell's account of her dream (pp. 115–16), as in Vardaman's relation of the river crossing (pp. 143–44), it leads to a leveling process in which words are reduced to a sort of verbal magma. It is noticeable however that all these devices are used sparingly in *As I Lay Dying,* and that the liberties taken with linguistic conventions never lead to complete nonsense. The sentence quoted above, "Pa shaves . . . ," becomes quite easy to understand once Vardaman's affective logic has been grasped by the reader. Similarly, in the passages without punctuation, the restitution of periods and commas would soon reestablish syntactic order. All these anomalies function essentially as signals; they never seriously compromise the readability of the novel.

Closely interwoven with the often loose syntax of the reported conversations and oral accounts, and with the broken, erratic patterns of the interior monologue proper, there is the fuller and firmer style, more elaborated in a traditional way—in a word, more "literary"—that is characteristic of most of the Darl sections. This extremely resourceful and flexible style can show on occasion remarkable sobriety and objectivity, as in this passage from the first section:

> Tull's wagon stands beside the spring, hitched to the rail, the reins wrapped about the seat stanchion. In the wagon bed are two chairs. Jewel stops at the spring and takes the gourd from the willow branch and drinks. I pass him and mount the path, beginning to hear Cash's saw. [p. 4]

Here we follow the movements of an eye which does not take in more than one aspect of reality at a time. As one critic notes, the passage consists of "a series of clear visual images, experienced immediately, in sequence as they occur in the passing moment of time."[5] No comment is added, no interpretation given; there is nothing but the sharply perceived particulars of the external scene.

Yet Darl's manner is not always so clipped and detached. It is in his monologues that the novelist's precise but enveloping style comes most often to the fore. The sentences are more varied and gain in length and complexity. Their variety is such that they cannot be reduced to a basic pattern. There are some recurrent features nonetheless, what one might call "structure in expansion": a simple statement—the account of an action or attitude—generally forms its kernel; grouped around this center are series of participles, present and/or past, either in apposition to the subject or object, or used as complements of circumstance. Here are two samples:

Leaning above the bed, her hands lifted a little, the fan still moving like it has for ten days, she begins to keen. [p. 47]

We stand there, leaning back against the current, watching the water where he disappeared, holding the dead rope between us like two men holding the nozzle of a fire hose, waiting for the water. [p. 153]

Although the examples given here are fairly short and simple, they may suffice to indicate Faulkner's well-known tendency to load his sentences with as much information as he can. The sentence not only names an action, it gives us in the same breath all the attendant circumstances and modalities; it tends to become the embryo of a scene or rather of a *tableau vivant,* for the proliferating participles stifle, as it were, the finite verb and freeze its motion into stasis. (Faulkner's fascination with arrested time, which will be discussed further in a later chapter, is thus knit into the very texture of his prose.) In many cases the same law of expansion also seems to apply to the composition of the paragraphs. A large number of paragraphs open with the brief notation of an action, followed by an exploration of the moment when the action occurred. The first sentence usually contains all the information needed to understand the narrative sequence, and in certain sections, as, for instance, section 12 (the death scene), it would be a simple matter of fitting paragraph openings together to have a synopsis of the whole scene.

Another prominent feature of Faulkner's style in *As I Lay Dying* is the use of parallelism, balance, and antithesis. This is how the novelist describes the carrying of the coffin:

It is light, yet they move slowly; empty, yet they carry it carefully; lifeless, yet they move with hushed precautionary words to one another. . . . [p. 75]

The parallelism of these three sentences underlines the contrast of the two clauses of which each is composed; at the same time the alternation of short clauses—elliptical from the second sentence on—and of increasingly long ones introduces a halting rhythm which prevents the effect from being one of stiff symmetry. The formal structure is there, but with its edges smoothed off to a subtly cadenced fluency and a quietly effective expressiveness. With a heavier beat, these parallel patterns also occur in Anse's musings on the aims of the Lord:

> When He aims for something to be always a-moving, He makes it longways, like a road or a horse or a wagon, but when He aims for something to stay put, He makes it up-and-down ways, like a tree or a man. [p. 35]

One could also quote Darl's speculations on the relationship between sleep, being, and not-being, in which the parallelism, accentuated by the anaphoric "And" is cast into a ternary scheme:

> And before you are emptied for sleep, what are you. And when you are emptied for sleep, you are not. And when you are filled with sleep, you never were. [p. 76]

In such developments, one finds in fact most of the characteristics of periodic style. In *As I Lay Dying,* this style, which could be illustrated as well by Peabody's considerations on death (cf. pp. 42–43) or by Addie's meditation on the vanity of words (cf. pp. 165–166), is essentially that of reflection. There is often something gnomic about it, something suggestive of a wisdom matured by long experience and distilled in cogent aphorisms. But even here Faulkner's language remains primarily a language of images and emotions. And when by chance it takes a more abstract turn, as in Darl's metaphysical exercises in conjugation, it appears more as a mimed dialectic, a sort of verbal gesticulation, than as the expression of ordered and fixed rational thought. This mimicry can become parody: Cash's incongruous catalogue (pp. 77–78) provides an example to be relished. Thought, it might seem, is summoned only to confess its ridiculous or pathetic impotence. Yet however incapable it is of establishing a meaningful order, this language forcibly suggests a certain vision of the world:

> It takes two people to make you, and one people to die. That's how the world is going to end. [p. 38]

Affirmations, abrupt and peremptory, follow one another with what seems to be the relentless logic of an irrefutable deduction. It is almost as if one were dealing with a syllogism (two premises and a conclusion). The appearance of rigor, however, is delusive: Darl's reflection startles us by its enigmatic, oracular transparency, but its clarity is not that of reasoning. It is to rhetoric, not to logical discourse, that it owes its eloquence.

RHETORIC

WITH Faulkner, rhetorical figures are not a simple ornament for discourse; they belong to the very tools of his art. "His medium," says Wright Morris, "is rhetoric, handled with such power that language spreads on the canvas like painting. In his hands it is a way of painting with words."[6] At its most flamboyant this rhetoric is rarely at its best; it is when the author's devices are best hidden that they prove most effective. In *As I Lay Dying* they are put at the service of vision (Darl) and of passion (Addie), and parody themselves in Anse's homespun philosophical lucubrations and in the Reverend Whitfield's outrageously biblical eloquence. But there is another kind of rhetoric, unprepared and untutored, a rhetoric in the raw in Dewey Dell's monologues:

> The signboard comes in sight. It is looking out at the road now, because it can wait. New Hope. 3 mi. it will say. New Hope. 3 mi. New Hope. 3 mi. And then the road will begin, curving away into the trees, empty with waiting, saying New Hope three miles.
>
> I heard that my mother is dead. I wish I had time to let her die. I wish I had time to wish I had. It is because in the wild and outraged earth too soon too soon too soon. It's not that I wouldn't and will not it's that it is too soon too soon too soon. [p. 114]

The immediate effect of such a passage is one of extreme randomness. There is nothing conventionally rhetorical about it, and yet, as Robert Humphrey has pointed out,[7] Dewey Dell's monologue displays a whole series of figures: personification ("It is *looking out* at the road now, because it can *wait*"—"the *wild* and *outraged* earth"), inversion ("New Hope. 3 mi. it will say"), repetition ("New Hope. 3 mi."—"I wish"—"too soon"), understatement ("I heard that my mother is dead"), anacoluthon and ellipsis ("It is because . . . too soon"), anaphora ("It is . . . It's not . . . it's that . . ."). What is most surprising is not the presence of this or that figure but that there should be so many in so short a fragment; "it is," as Humphrey puts it, "the piling up of them, the over-all use of *incrementum* that is unique and that, because it indicates a need for close reading and gives an enigmatic tone to the passage, serves to heighten the effect of the privacy of the materials."[8]

Now except for the passages of plain conversation and straightforward narrative prose, this density holds good for the whole novel. Throughout *As I Lay Dying* Faulkner's style is astonishingly rich in rhetorical figures. We have already noted the variety of sentence patterns, but one cannot fail to be struck too by the extraordinary profusion of tropes. With Faulkner it is rare for words to retain their literal meaning right to the end. Diverted from their initial function, divested of their usual associations, drawn into a play of substitution (metaphors, metonymies), or else set alongside other words with which they have no natural affinity but whose contagious effect they nonetheless suffer (hypallages, oxymorons), they are subjected to so many manipulations and charged with such a mass of connotations and nuances that they almost generate a semantic system of their own.

It should be added that the language spoken by Faulkner's farmers already constitutes a fund of figures in its own right. For the most part, they are ordinary figures of speech lacking in any originality, but subtly revived in the context of the novel by the writer's art, they often acquire a new and meaningful freshness. As an example, let us take an expression which often features in *As I Lay Dying:* "flesh and blood." Rhetorical treatises would have called it a synecdoche of matter, flesh and blood designating the family in its organic reality. This synecdoche is used by three people in the book: Cora (p. 21), Anse (pp. 99, 218), Addie (p. 165). As Anse and Cora are characters diametrically opposed to Addie, the repetition of the phrase produces an ironical effect: for the first two it is merely a way of putting it, one cliché among others in their hollow rhetoric; for Addie on the other hand it refers to a way of feeling and living, and "flesh and blood" are certainly more than mere words to her. In her monologue, moreover, the use of these terms corresponds more often than not to a figure other than synecdoche. The meaning of "blood" is not restricted simply to progeny, and when she speaks of the "red bitter blood boiling through the land" (p. 166) she makes it a metaphor of life itself.[9]

Metaphor is the figure of figures in *As I Lay Dying*. It is consubstantial with the vision and art of the novelist. Of all the demons which presided over Faulkner's work, the demon of analogy was without doubt one of the most intrusive, and in this novel his presence is as strongly felt as in any other. Through the multiplicity of unexpected connections and reverberations they introduce into the book, metaphors reinforce the interrelatedness of its parts; by carrying its meanings beyond literal significance, they expand the fictional world beyond the narrow boundaries of realistic convention and make room for the imagination. Their function within the novel's texture is very similar to that of the symbols within its structure: both are intended to transmute the factual-objective into the poetic.

In dealing with the setting of the book, we shall see more precisely how metaphorization works, and what transfers and exchanges are made possible by its agency. Some of its modali-

ties might however be noted here. Almost any word may serve
as a starting point: a noun ("the furious *tide* of Jewel's despair,"
p. 92), a verb ("The sound of the saw *snores* steadily into the
room," p. 51), a participle (*"dressed* in sin," pp. 166, 167),
an adjective (*"mournful* water," p. 135), or an adverb ("her
pole-thin body clings *furiously* . . . ," p. 91). Figurative language is likely to occur anywhere, almost at random; it may be
induced by a chance word, just as it can spring from a tele-
scoping of sensations (synesthesia), as in some of the Vardaman sections: "I can see hearing coil towards him, caressing,
shaping his hard shape" (p. 55).

Often analogy is also expressed through comparisons. These
doubtless do not have the suggestive compactness and abrupt
beauty of pure metaphor. They set side by side what a metaphor
compresses into a single image. Their more discursive character,
however, gives greater extension and an almost explanatory
value to the correspondences they reveal. In Faulkner's work,
similes are almost a stylistic tic. Flaubert once wrote to Louise
Colet: "I am eaten up by similes as one is by fleas, and I spend
all my time crushing them; my sentences are teeming with
them."[10] Faulkner could have said as much, except that to some
extent he was quite willing to let himself be eaten, and so unlike
Flaubert, followed the natural bent of his genius. In *As I Lay
Dying* similes abound and all the characters without exception
use them on occasion. Among the farmers, bucolic comparisons
clearly prevail. They are both familiar and unexpected: Tull
compares the women's conversation to "bees murmuring in a
water bucket" (p. 82), Cora makes him think of "a jar of milk
in the spring" (p. 132), and elsewhere, in a surprising four-
pronged simile, he links Whitfield and his voice with two horses
crossing a ford (p. 86).

In the Darl sections the range of analogies is wider. Many
of them are taken from nature and country life, but references
are also made to other fields, such as painting and sculpture.

Thus Darl likens Jewel and Gillespie struggling in the burning barn to "two figures in a Greek frieze" (p. 211) and compares the coffin on the sawhorse to a "cubistic bug" (p. 209)—rather unlikely similes coming from a bumpkin like him. On the whole, Darl's comparisons also stand out because of their length. They may relate only to nouns, but very often they take the form of subordinate clauses introduced by *as though* or *as if,* and sometimes there are two or three of these comparative-conditional clauses in a single sentence:

> Cash labors about the trestles, moving back and forth, lifting and placing the planks with long clattering reverberations in the dead air *as though* he were lifting and dropping them at the bottom of an invisible well, the sounds ceasing without departing, *as if* any movement might dislodge them from the immediate air in reverberant repetition. [pp. 71–72]

Addie's monologue likewise presents a remarkable concentration of metaphors and similes. Consider, for example, this passage:

> hearing the dark voicelessness in which the words are the deeds, and the other words that are not the deeds, that are just the gaps in peoples' [*sic*] lacks, coming down like the cries of the geese out of the wild darkness in the old terrible nights, fumbling at the deeds like orphans to whom are pointed out in a crowd two faces and told, That is your father, your mother. [p. 166]

Oxymoron ("hearing . . . voicelessness"), synesthesia ("dark voicelessness"), words/deeds antithesis presented in the form of antanaclasis ("words" taken first figuratively then literally), metaphor ("other words" equated with "gaps"), double simile ("the cries of the geese"—"orphans"), here again we find a very singular interlacing of figures. It is paralleled by the intricacy of the syntax, marked by the alternation of relatives and participles in apposition, and gathering itself in increasing masses, true to the principle of expansion basic to Faulkner's style, which we have already seen working in simpler sentence patterns: the first complement to "hearing" is prolonged by a relative clause, the second by two relatives to which are added two circumstantial comparisons the second of which, more fully dramatized and developed than the first, gives rise (after the image of the orphans) to the sketch of a little scene—a fiction in a nutshell, which could become the starting point of another story and another novel.

For the analysis of such a passage as this to be complete, one would need to study the subtle interplay of rhythms (the antithetical balancing of the first two relative clauses, the brief scornful hammering of "the gaps in peoples' lacks," the long sliding movement of "coming down . . . nights," the brusque halt at the end) and of recurrent sounds (the repetition of words, assonances like *deeds-geese, gaps-lacks, wild-nights*). Throughout the novel Faulkner uses sound and rhythm patterns: their particular expressiveness supplements the effects of the tropes and other rhetorical devices. It seems as if the writer were trying to correct the arbitrary nature of verbal signs by eliciting meaning from the very sound and substance of the words themselves. Thus the weighty polysyllables and hard consonants of three adjectives make the as yet distant threat of the buzzards seem much nearer:

From here they are no more than s*peck*s, im*pl*a*c*able, *p*atient, *p*or-*t*en*t*ous. [p. 88]

Elsewhere Faulkner has recourse to imitative effects. Sometimes they are simple onomatopeias, like the triple "Chuck" of the adze at the end of the first section (p. 5) or the triple "whish" suggesting the flutter of the fans during the funeral service (p. 81). At the beginning of the storm, a patter of monosyllables makes us hear the brutal fall of the first raindrops:

The first harsh, sparse, swift drops rush through the leaves. . . . [p. 72]

Often Faulkner also uses these homophonic effects for a sustained final chord. Thus one of Dewey Dell's sections ends with:

> I feel like a wet seed wild in the hot blind earth. [p. 61]

The metaphor of the seed, with all the sense impressions—wetness, heat, blindness—enveloping it, is here amplified by the long vowels (i) and diphthong sounds (aɪ), the liquidity of the consonants (four *l*s), the use of alliteration (*wet-wild*) and assonance (*feel-seed, wild-blind*): the whole sentence reverberates like a long plaintive cry. One of Darl's monologues ends likewise with an elegiac coda:

> How often have I lain beneath rain on a strange roof, thinking of home. [p. 76]

In the last examples quoted, nothing separates Faulkner's prose from poetry. It has poetry's concentrated energy and indefinite powers of suggestion. But in *As I Lay Dying,* as in all Faulkner's great novels, poetry is not only present in these unexpected flashes of lyricism. The whole novel tends toward being a poem. From diction to syntax, from syntax to rhetoric with its rich array of figures, metaphors, sonorities, and rhythms, Faulkner's style is always on the alert, prodigiously active and creative. And it is above all in its irrepressible vitality and nimble inventiveness that it is related to poetic usage. Forging new words or forcing old ones into new uses, twisting syntax into startling patterns of his own making, drawing at the same time upon the resources of colloquialism and of literary tradition, and freely mingling high rhetoric with low prose, Faulkner is ceaselessly reshaping language for his own ends. No wonder then that language in turn begins to *work,* to ferment, to take on a new life and reacquire its old magical properties. A system of dead signs—"dead sounds" as Addie calls them in the novel—becomes a living network of symbols, a full and vibrant image of the world, an epiphany of reality.

4

Technique

Technically the most striking feature of *As I Lay Dying* is Faulkner's use of the interior monologue. The same device had already been used in *The Sound and the Fury,* yet its effects on the narrative are markedly different in the two novels. In *The Sound and the Fury* its implementation leads to the shattering of the traditional framework of narration; in *As I Lay Dying,* on the other hand, the author's reliance on interior monologue and the extreme fragmentation of viewpoints in no way prevent the novel from being a *narrative* in the accepted sense of the term, namely, the account of a series of events given coherence by the unity of a single line of action.

As I Lay Dying is in this respect one of Faulkner's simpler works. Unlike most of his other novels, it does not disrupt the basic chronology of events nor does its narrative indulge in digressions. With a few hardly perceptible exceptions, the unity of action is respected from start to finish and the whole tale is perfectly circumscribed in space and time.

These are the space and time of a *journey:* the space is measured by the distance separating the country from the town, the Bundrens' house in the hills from Jefferson, the end of their trek;

the time is the ten days they need to prepare and undertake their journey. *As I Lay Dying* is first and foremost the account of an expedition. The journey determines both the theme and the form of the book. As well as constituting one of the focal points of the novel's meanings,[1] it provides the narrative with one of its main organizing principles.

As is the case with most travel accounts, the novel consists of a series of episodes. The preparation and departure, the river crossing, the barn fire, the arrival at Jefferson—these are the major sections of the tale. They are presented in their time sequence. Manipulation of them occurs primarily, as we shall see, in the distribution and orchestration of narrative voices; it hardly affects the narrative itself, whose arrangement remains broadly chronological. It will also be noted that like any episodic novel, *As I Lay Dying* shows little plotting. In a sense, the action certainly results from the development of the initial situation, namely the Bundrens' obligation to go and bury Addie in Jefferson cemetery, but neither the mishaps of the journey nor their succession are predetermined by that situation. Among the obstacles they meet on the way, some are purely fortuitous (the swollen river, the broken bridges, losing the mules, Cash's accident) and others are brought about voluntarily by human agency (the barn fire started by Darl), but the episodes arising from the confrontation with these obstacles are not linked by any requirement inherent in the logic of the tale itself. Their order could be reversed, their number increased or decreased, without its structure's being seriously altered.

From this seeming looseness one should not, however, leap to the conclusion that the narrative lacks cohesion. Cohesion is guaranteed by the permanence of the *dramatis personae* as well as by the converging motivations which prompt them into undertaking the adventure. The journey of the Bundrens is no random wandering along chance paths. It is an expedition undertaken for precise reasons: for Addie, it is the realization of a wish—to be buried at Jefferson—and perhaps too a posthumous act of revenge (cf. pp. 164–65); for the family as a group, it is the fulfillment of a promise. To these, private motives are added—a new set of teeth and a new wife for Anse, an abortion for Dewey Dell, a "graphophone" for Cash, bananas and an electric train for Vardaman—motives which, in spite of their disparity, strengthen the Bundrens' determination to go to Jefferson, but whose self-interested nature throws suspicion on the act of family piety they are supposed to be accomplishing. Yet two of Addie's children—Jewel and Darl—are notable exceptions in this respect: Jewel's personal motivation coincides exactly with the official reason for the journey; Darl, on the other hand, stands out from the rest of the family by his indifference, then by his hostility to the project, and he is the only one who tries at one point to prevent its being carried out. Both of them perform an essential function in the narrative strategy of the author: the first appears as the main *hero* of the story, the one whose fierce energy pushes the action forward and whose exploits and sacrifices allow the enterprise to succeed; the second, because of his critical detachment, assumes in essence the peripheral role of *narrator* or, as one critic has aptly put it, of *antiheroic intelligence*.[2]

Finally it should be noted that at the center of *As I Lay Dying*, of its structure and of its themes, lies the figure, at once present and absent, of Addie Bundren, the "I" of the book's title. If the *narrative* apparently follows the linear progression appropriate to a journey, the *novel* is ordered according to a circular scheme focused on this figure. This scheme in some ways brings to mind the one Henry James has diagrammed in his Preface to *The Awkward Age:*

> I drew on a sheet of paper . . . the neat figure of a circle consisting of a number of small rounds disposed at equal distance about a central object. The central object was my situation, my subject in itself, to which the thing would owe its title, and the small rounds represented so many distinct lamps, as I liked to call them, the

function of each of which would be to light with all due intensity one of its aspects.[3]

The central object here is Addie's corpse both as a material thing, as the constant mainspring of and object at stake in the physical action, and in its symbolic function, as a reminder of the event which has just upset the existence of the Bundrens, as a visible sign of the great void left by Addie's death, which each member of the family after his fashion tries to fill. As for the circle, it is made up of all those still alive who gather around the body, suddenly brought face to face with the enigma of death. Each consciousness caught in the novel's sweep is one of those little lamps of which James speaks; each one, in its flickering light, illuminating one particular aspect of the central figure and situation. But instead of lamps one might also suggest a comparison with reflecting mirrors: most of the sections, in addition to throwing an oblique and intermittent light on Addie's personality, testify to the persistent effects of her dark radiance. It is precisely in terms of reciprocal illumination that one could define the relationship between Addie's single monologue and the rest of the novel. Were it not for this monologue, the book would lack focus, and much of its meaning would be lost on the reader, since the family drama can be understood only by reference to the personal tragedy suggested by the dead woman's confession. But conversely Addie's monologue needs the echoing space of the whole work for its significance to be fully grasped.

A double movement is thus set up. On the one hand, within the circle there is a simultaneous centrifugal and centripetal movement, a nonstop to-ing and fro-ing between circle and center; on the other hand, there is a circular movement governing the whole novel and making it turn around its fixed axis. Similar dynamics can be observed in Faulkner's earlier novels: *Soldiers' Pay* was conceived as a sort of last vigil turning on Donald Mahon, the dying hero; *The Sound and the Fury* revolved around the absent-present figure of Caddy Compson, the "lost girl." *As I Lay Dying* turns likewise around Addie and her death, and the rapid shift of viewpoint, with its recurrences and reverberations, introduces this gyration into the very structure of the novel.

That this circular pattern possesses thematic significance hardly needs to be stressed. In this connection it is interesting to note that the circle also appears in the imagery of the novel. The whole story of the journey is punctuated by the repeated evocation of the circles traced in the sky by the buzzards which follow the funeral cortège, and the circling vultures ceaselessly intersecting the straight line of the Bundrens' progression could almost be seen as an emblem[4] of the book's structure. In addition, it is significant that Darl associates his dead mother with a wheel: "the red road lies like a spoke of which Addie Bundren is the rim" (p. 102). In her soliloquy Addie herself refers to the circle of her solitude; by Cash's birth, she remarks, her "aloneness had been violated and then made whole again by the violation: time, Anse, love, what you will, outside the circle" (p. 164). The metaphor of the circle would apply almost equally well to most of the other Bundrens: each time one of them voices his thoughts and feelings, he becomes for a while, to borrow another of James's phrases, "the central intelligence" of the novel, and each time his inner speech is enclosed by the circle of his private desires and secret obsessions—a circle of self-absorption and solitude he is either unwilling or unable to break. If the pattern of *As I Lay Dying* suggests first of all a moving circle whose center is Addie, it could also be described as a series of waves and eddies: it is as if a handful of pebbles were thrown into still water, rippling its surface, making concentric circles which overlap and interact in unexpected ways as they expand.

Both narrative and novel, then, have their own structure. In spatial terms the difference is that between a straight line and a circle. Yet this opposition is obviously too crudely stated not to require qualification. In fact narrative structure and fictional structure do not exist independent of each other: the latter contains the former, the novel envelops the narrative and ends by changing its course. Although linear in its basic development, the story seems nonetheless to describe a double loop. The first of these loops is Addie's journey, a return journey which takes the dead woman back to the place of her birth. The second comes full circle at the very end of the novel, when Anse introduces his new wife to his children: "Meet Mrs. Bundren" (p. 250). Present at the beginning, Mrs. Bundren had gradually moved further away until she finally disappeared in Jefferson cemetery. Here she is back again. Certainly she is not the same at all. But by replacing Addie, who is dead and buried and has now left her family for good, the new Mrs. Bundren comes along to occupy a place left vacant. From life to death, from death to life, the cycle is closed (and at the same time open to the possibility of other returns and reversals), and the ending sends us back to the beginning. But not quite: the closing situation reproduces the opening one, but in another, lower key. The substitution is like a usurpation; the pop-eyed, duck-shaped new Mrs. Bundren is only Addie's grotesque understudy. And the whole journey suggests a process of degradation, best symbolized by the increasingly repulsive smell of the rotting corpse. Cash's gangrenous broken leg gets worse and worse in its cement cast; Dewey Dell, frustrated in her efforts to get an abortion and seduced by a drugstore clerk, will bear her bastard child; Jewel, badly burned by the fire, loses his treasured horse. The tensions within the family reach their climax in Dewey Dell's and Jewel's murderous assault on Darl. Darl himself goes mad and is finally disowned—the replacement of the mother thus coinciding with the repudiation of one of her sons. Ironically, Anse is the only one to gain something by the adventure.

Perhaps it is the figure of the spiral which best indicates the repetition-with-a-difference. *As I Lay Dying* carries us along in a helical movement or, more exactly, down in a spinning dive. The end of the narrative draws near its starting point and at that very moment veers away. Everything starts again and nothing is the same. The end of the novel is a false restoration (just as Anse's new teeth are false), a ludicrous dénouement echoing with Darl's mad laughter: ambiguity is given a final twist and irony is raised to its highest pitch.

TIME AND TENSE

STORYTELLERS generally resort to the past tense because it provides them with the maneuvering room they need to organize the data of their story into a coherent perspective. Now in *As I Lay Dying* Faulkner most often uses the *present,* a tense apparently more appropriate to drama than to fiction. The distance between narration and narrated is reduced here to a minimum, and the two tend to become virtually simultaneous. In the first section of the novel, Darl tells us what he is doing when he is doing it, what he sees when he sees it, so that there is no hiatus between the event, the perceiving consciousness, and the process of verbalization. The discourse of the novel is assumed to be contemporaneous with the reality—or, if you prefer, the fiction—it presents to the reader; it purports to be its immediate, moment-by-moment transcription. Unlike conventional narrative, *As I Lay Dying* does not move from a more or less distant past toward a closer past or toward the present. Nor is there any question, as in some of Faulkner's novels, of starting from the present (of the hero or the narrator) to grope backward in time, of radiating from the hub of a memory in action. Whatever the point reached in the course of reading, it coincides most often with the "now" of a vision and an action: we are in the present, we share it with the hero-narrators of the story, associated with both an action and a narrative in progress.

Yet, unless the novelist uses the dramatic mode exclusively, it is extremely difficult to handle present-tense narration consistently throughout, and one has to admit that Faulkner has not always avoided the pitfalls of his method. Some of the temporal inconsistencies may be attributed simply to oversight; most of them, however, seem to derive directly from the limitations of the tense chosen.

In *As I Lay Dying* narrative and fictional time tend to converge, and they do in fact occasionally coincide (particularly in the dialogues of which Faulkner makes lavish use throughout the novel), but the narrative is not thereby freed from the constraints and artifices governing all narration. First, to begin with the most obvious, one should note that the (fictional or fictive) duration of the recorded events extends over ten days whereas the (real) time required to read the book is some two or three hours. This disparity alone precludes the possibility of total correspondence between the time of narration and the time of action, and so imposes the need for compression. Furthermore, the very division of the novel into relatively short sections and the constant shifts from one narrator to another imply a principle of discontinuity: what we are given is a rapid montage of contrasting snapshots rather than the smooth record of a continuous time flow.

While playing on effects of alternation and changes of tack, Faulkner nonetheless sought, in the first half of the book especially, to weld the sections firmly together. Thus the first fifteen sections (with the exception of the sixth) present an almost unbroken sequence despite the frequent changes of viewpoint. Not that their succession corresponds to a strict chronological order; there may be some overlapping between several consecutive sections, but on the whole each one carries the narrative that much forward. Continuity is assured by the attention the novelist pays to the development of the physical action and to its setting: the characters move in a carefully circumscribed space (the house and its immediate surroundings), and the reader has no trouble following them from one section to the next as they come and go (consider, for example, Darl's or Jewel's movements in the first five sections). It no doubt happens that when Faulkner takes us from one consciousness to another we are baffled by the sudden change of outlook, but at no point does the thread of the narrative break, and by the very switching of viewpoints the narration unquestionably makes up in vividness and variety what it may lose in clarity.

In these early sections, all the action hangs on the imminence of Addie's death; it follows a rising curve to the climactic death scene described by Darl in section 12. The whole narrative is organized around a number of great *scenes* (Addie's death, the river crossing, etc.). In other words, we are dealing here with *dramatized* time, stressed and unstressed alternately. During the stressed periods, the present of narration tends to expand, to fuse with that of fiction, and the narrative slows down in consequence. During the unstressed periods on the other hand, the present contracts and, as we shall see, sometimes gives way to the past, thus speeding up the narrative. It becomes clear therefore that far from basing the narration on the uniform passage of a continuous present, Faulkner subjects it to different tempos, each variation being a function of the dramatic and/or thematic importance of the narrative sequence in question.

The narrative makes the slowest progress in the first nineteen sections; they correspond to the first of the ten days recounted in the novel, to the hours before and after Addie's death. Thus the first day alone occupies almost a third of the book. As this day represents only a tenth of the total duration of the action, it takes up a disproportionate amount of space in comparison with the rest, and particularly in comparison with the next two days, which are dealt with in very few pages (sect. 20–21, pp. 80–89).[5] In the account of the journey itself, the general pace of the narrative is quicker than in the opening sections, with a marked acceleration towards the end. But here too there is no constant proportion between the objective time-unit (the day) and the corresponding narrative sequence in the novel. Certain days, notably the sixth and the seventh, are summarily passed over (sect. 43–44, pp. 175–187; Armstid's account in section 43 covers three days: the end of the fifth, the sixth, and the beginning of the seventh). The others are presented at greater length and more directly: the fourth, eighth, and ninth days each take up seven or eight sections, and the longest account is devoted to the fifth (twelve sections: the end of 29, 30–38, 42, and the beginning of 43), the day of the river crossing, the climax of the journey.

It is quite evident that this dramatization is not compatible with the exclusive use of the present tense. The present is perfectly appropriate for reporting the scenes of action, where events are shown as they happen. But as soon as it becomes necessary to make time elapse, to link scenes to one another, to span whole days in a few pages or even lines, the novelist has to fall back on retrospective narration. *As I Lay Dying* is no exception to this rule. The present is far from being the only tense used by Faulkner. The manuscript shows, indeed, that he was aware of the difficulties involved in his narrative mode and sometimes hesitated between present and past.[6] In fact, out of the fifty-nine sections, only twenty-four are written in the present, and there are many in which past and present are interspersed (the shifts being marked at times, as in *The Sound and the Fury,* by the use of italics), and some twenty may be counted where the past clearly predominates.

More often than not, the past recalled is a recent past: in most of the sections attributed to characters outside the Bundren family, the narrator's present is only slightly later than the time of the events related. Yet *As I Lay Dying* also contains a number of *flashbacks* which reveal scenes and events prior to the current action. Sometimes they are extremely brief: Darl's childhood memories (pp. 10–11), snatches of conversation between Anse and Addie (p. 36), the recollection of Dewey Dell's dream (pp. 115–16); at other times memory lingers over the past, reminiscences coalesce and then come to form episodes in retrospect embedded within the narrative of the present. Thus Dewey Dell recalls the circumstances of her seduction by Lafe (pp. 25–26); Darl recounts at length how Jewel paid for his spotted horse, creeping out every night for months to work in a neighbor's field (pp. 121–29); Cora reports a conversation about sin and salvation she once had with Addie (pp. 158–59). When these past episodes are directly connected to the present situation or are induced by traceable mental associations (cf. p. 10), the shift from present to past comes quite naturally and the continuity of the narrative is scarcely broken. The case is different when the retrospection occupies a complete section with no reference whatever to the present. Considerable uncertainty then arises, since the reader finds it impossible to locate the narrator in time. This uncertainty is conspicuous in one of the Cora sections (sect. 39, pp. 158–60) and in the Whitfield section (sect. 41, pp. 169–71); it is even more baffling in Addie's monologue (sect. 40, pp. 161–68). A narrative within the narrative from which the novel derives both its light and its obscurity, Addie's confession, crucial as it is to an understanding of the book, is quite unwarranted from the point of view of verisimilitude since, when she starts to speak, Addie has been dead for five days. Not only has her monologue no immediate logical connection with the current action but also there is no way of locating it in space and time. The voice we hear in it is timeless and bodiless, conjured up by the author's necromancy.[7]

If section 40 appears to be a flagrant breach of the code of realism, the basic principle of the flashback technique in no way contravenes it. Once the convention of the interior monologue is established, it is natural to allow the remembrance of things past to replace at times the perception of the present moment. No major difficulty is involved either in supposing the time of narration to be occasionally later than that of the action (although this assumption makes it hard to tell immediate present from historical present).[8] On the other hand, it is difficult to admit that a narrative system of which the present constitutes the referential axis should allow events to be alluded to before they happen. Now, as one critic has pointed out,[9] the novel includes a number of *anticipations* for which there is no justification unless the narrators are credited with the faculty of foretelling the future. Thus whereas Addie's death occurs in section 12 and the journey does not begin until section 22, Cora refers to her neighbor's dying moments in section 6 and reflects that Addie "was not cold in the coffin before they were carting her forty miles away to bury her" (p. 21). Similarly, Tull (sect. 16, 20, 36), Moseley (sect. 45), and Mac-Gowan (sect. 55) recapitulate events before they actually happen, and Cash twice mentions the second "Mrs. Bundren" at a time when nobody other than Anse knows she is to become his wife (cf. p. 225). These inconsistencies and anachronisms may be partially explained by the speed with which *As I Lay Dying* was written. They are perhaps regrettable, but it would be going too far to say that they seriously compromise the narrative's credibility.

A further problem Faulkner had to solve was that of *simultaneity*. As long as the action is unified and all the actors are grouped together, there is no difficulty, but as soon as it splits into parallel actions occurring in different places, it seems out of the question for a single narrator to take them immediately into account. Faulkner evades the difficulty by resorting to an artifice: he endows Darl, one of his principal narrators, with the gift of preternatural clairvoyance, which allows him to report two scenes at the same time. In section 3, for example, Darl describes what Jewel is doing with his horse in the pasture behind the barn although Darl is near the porch talking with his father. This weird ubiquity is even more striking in section 12, where Darl gives a circumstantial account of Addie's death, or in section 17, where he imagines Cash working on the coffin during the rainstorm, both scenes being reported while he is on the road with Jewel, miles from home.

These further breaches of verisimilitude cannot however be

ascribed to the novelist's carelessness or imputed to his arbitrary whims. Like Addie's posthumous monologue, Darl's occasional second sight is indeed a challenge to the conventions of realistic narrative. Yet in order to understand the liberties Faulkner takes with them, it is necessary to look beyond the narrative and inquire into their meaning within the total context of the novel.

POINTS OF VIEW

FAULKNER'S refusal to be confined within the role of the traditional storyteller and to play the narrative game according to established rules and his determination to bend everything to the law of his own will are also reflected in the sovereign freedom with which he manages the possibilities offered by the manipulation of point of view.

Earlier, in *The Sound and the Fury,* Faulkner had resorted to a fragmented point of view. In *As I Lay Dying* this fragmentation is taken a stage further: instead of four sections, there are fifty-nine. They are of varying importance, but never very long (the average is 2 to 4 pages, the maximum 7, the shortest a mere 5 words), and are shared among fifteen different narrators. The distribution is as follows: Darl 19, Vardaman 10, Vernon Tull 6, Cash 5, Dewey Dell 4, Cora Tull 3, Anse 3, Peabody 2, Addie 1, Jewel 1, Whitfield 1, Samson 1, Armstid 1, Moseley 1, Mac-Gowan 1. Seven of the narrators belong to the Bundren family (actor-narrators); the eight others are outsiders, either episodic participants in the action or mere witnesses (spectator-narrators). Yet if the two categories of narrators are numerically almost equal, the share of sections given to the Bundrens (43) is far in excess of that of the outsiders (16). It is noteworthy, too, that Darl, with nineteen sections, takes on single-handed one-third of the narrative and thus occupies a highly privileged position as narrator.

One of the effects of this multiple point of view upon the

reader is that he is prevented from identifying himself with any one narrator. The shifts are too frequent to permit his settling to a single point of view. *The Sound and the Fury* plunged us into the stream of consciousness of Benjy, Quentin, and Jason in turn, and the immersions lasted long enough for the reader to adopt (and forget) the point of view of the narrator. In *As I Lay Dying* these immersions are too short; the stream does not carry one with it. The broken construction of the novel keeps the reader at a distance and puts him in the position of a spectator rather than of a participant, thus preventing the emotional involvement generally associated with the interior monologue. Faulkner was nonetheless at pains to retain some unity of vision by making Darl his principal narrator and setting him—rather like Quentin Compson in *Absalom, Absalom!*—at the point of junction between narrative and novel. Although he is only given a third of the narration, his detachment and insight, his gifts of observation and expression, and his faculty of second sight single him out quite naturally for the function of "central intelligence."[10] Like the dramatized narrators in Conrad and James, Darl is the one who sees and knows the most, and it is through him that we are most completely, if not most reliably, informed, not only of the external development of the action but also of the secret links which bind the Bundrens together and of the hidden motivations which guide their behavior.

At the same time, Darl's monologues tell us about Darl himself, about his reveries and obsessions and about his vain quest for identity. A two-way mirror, each section reflects external events as well as their impact upon a consciousness; each section strives to link up with the object of the narration—the story of which it is presumed to be a fragment—and tends at the same time to flow back to its source, to be reabsorbed into the narrator's voice. What counts here at least as much as what is said is the word itself, the use made of it by each person and the sort of relay race in which it is passed from one to the other. The use of interior monologue

—a point of view which at any given moment betrays itself as such—has the effect of splitting the novel between the impersonality of *history* and the subjectivity of *discourse*.[11] There is a twofold subjectivity, both of a linguistic order (indicated by the constant recourse to the personal pronoun "I" and the predominance of the present tense) and of a psychological order, since in its essence the *interior* monologue, as it has been understood since Joyce, claims paradoxically to be an immediate transcription of prelogical or even preverbal mental processes.

In *As I Lay Dying,* however, the form taken by the interior monologue seldom fully corresponds to such a definition. If Faulkner uses the monologue as an instrument of psychological revelation, he also gives it a narrative function. In most of the sections one finds therefore differently weighted combinations of narrative and discursive elements. Among the narrative elements are accounts of current and past actions and reported conversations; among the discursive elements are descriptions, reflections, and comments made by the narrators, and everything pertaining to interior discourse as such (reveries, recollections, fantasies). There is, of course, no clear dividing line between these two areas. In the Darl sections especially only a closely detailed textual analysis would allow one to discriminate between narrative and nonnarrative components (cf. sect. 3, 10, 12, 34, 46, 57). In other sections, however, they are not so inextricably interwoven, and according to the dominant category one might make a distinction between the monologues whose function is essentially narrative and those which are primarily psychological in character and interest.

The first are used either to relate a scene as it happens or to link different moments of the action and unite them in a coherent perspective. Darl is the character most often responsible for direct, moment-to-moment reporting and for giving us a sense of participation in the action as it develops. Among the Bundrens, Darl and, to a lesser extent, Cash, who takes over towards the end of the novel, are alone in assuming in any real sense the function of narrators. Beside them, marginal to the action, are all the characters who form the chorus: Vernon and Cora Tull, Samson, Armstid, Peabody, Moseley, and MacGowan. They are there not so much to give us objective views as to provide a broader perspective, a wider frame of reference. The sections allotted to them are much more like dramatic soliloquies than interior monologues; they are in fact more often than not retrospective accounts in the first person. Meant for the ear rather than the eye, they sound like oral accounts, freely improvised, with the colloquial tone, the repetitiveness, and the fumbling prolixity of unpremeditated talk. Furthermore, as we have already noted, they are "spoken" in a vernacular idiom whose lexical and syntactic resources are exploited by the author with brilliant ingenuity. One therefore constantly feels the presence of the narrator's voice. And not only does each narrator's speech connote his social and geographical background but, far from being neutral, each witness reacts to the Bundrens' adventures according to his own temperament (perplexity tempered with neighborly kindness in the case of the farmers, a mixture of compassion and indignation in Doctor Peabody, self-righteous reproof in Cora Tull and Rachel Samson, outraged respectability in Moseley, cynical amusement in MacGowan), comments on them, and explains them according to his own lights (which are not always the right ones, as is amply shown by Cora's misinterpretations in section 6). As a group all these characters represent the rural community they belong to; they are its spokesmen, harboring its virtues and prejudices; they embody respectability confronted with scandal, collective wisdom challenged by the Bundrens' folly. Through their mingled voices the anonymous voice of the community is heard with its rules and values—an indispensable reference which, as always with Faulkner, emphasizes the opposition between social and individual, public and private.

Passing from the monologues of these outsiders to those of

the Bundrens, one finds a change of scale, a sharper focus, and more frequent close-ups. Simplifying, one might say that a view from within replaces one from without. The heroes of the novel are no longer seen from a distance; their story is no longer related by third parties. They themselves come and say what happens to them. But can they? In point of fact, most of the Bundrens are too directly involved in the journey, too busy acting, too much absorbed by their thoughts and emotions to be in a position to give an ordered account of what they are living through. Therefore there is a great deal more subjectivity in the sections attributed to them. The interest shifts from narration to narrator and from narrator to character, discourse takes precedence over narrative, and insofar as the latter persists, the way in which events impinge on the consciousness asserts itself to the detriment of their objective reality. One may also note that the differentiation of points of view is effected here both more distinctly and more subtly: each viewpoint is determined conjointly by the character's supposed degree of consciousness, by his psychological makeup, and by the mood of the moment.

Of these points of view, Darl's is by far the most flexible and complex. Darl, as we have seen, is the principal narrator, but his monologues are far from being a mere record of events. Nothing is less objective than his narrative. Its transparency is almost constantly blurred by the welter of descriptive touches, epithets, comparisons, and metaphors; images, thoughts, and memories well up at every turn of the narration, sometimes bursting out with short-lived brilliance, sometimes lingering for meditation and reverie. Darl's mind is so supple and fluid that it slips effortlessly from one thing to another and changes place and time in a trice. Consider, for example, section 3 (pp. 10–13): the very short opening paragraph is both descriptive (of Tull and Anse sitting on the back porch) and narrative (with Darl dipping his gourd into the water bucket to drink); a conversation is started by Anse's question to Darl ("Where's Jewel?"), but the answer is delayed for a page by the past suddenly breaking in on the present ("When I was a boy . . ."). Darl, drinking, reflects on the taste of water and remembers scenes from his childhood. The return to the present is marked by a close-up on "Pa's feet," the narrative is resumed ("I fling the dipper dregs . . .") and the question about Jewel is finally answered (" 'Down to the barn,' I say. 'Harnessing the team' "), Darl's answer inducing the superb description of Jewel and his horse on which the section ends. Darl's mind is seen working in four registers—perception, reflection, memory, and second sight—and passing from one to another with no other logic than the unpredictable one of mental association. Not all his monologues, to be sure, contain so many breaks and bifurcations. Yet all he says and describes bears the hallmark of an intensely personal vision. Almost every time Darl starts speaking, reality is transmuted: space begins to waver, the scenery takes on a disturbing life of its own, and everything stands out against an indistinct and shifting background with the strange clear-cut quality and fierce colors of a bad dream.

Hyperconscious and hypersensitive, Darl is almost always perfectly at ease with language. There is even in him a kind of intoxication with words. The same is not true of the younger Bundrens, Jewel, Dewey Dell, and, particularly, Vardaman. In them, the interior monologue sinks to a darker zone of greater confusion. It seeks to reflect the gropings of a nascent language, to capture the scarcely perceptible whispers and whimpers of a bemused consciousness which has difficulty in collecting itself around the kernel of a stable self. Neither Jewel nor Dewey Dell nor Vardaman is master of his words and all three have only a very dim and deformed awareness of the events with which they are confronted. If Darl's point of view has the broadest scope, theirs is certainly the most restricted. Jewel is all turbulence and action; only once does he break his silence, and his brief monologue peppered with invective and breathless with rage reveals nothing but his hatred of the others and his jealous love of Addie. As for Dewey Dell,

everything for her centers on the obsession with her body, her
pregnancy and intended abortion. In her monologues, and notably in sections 14 and 30, there is neither articulate thought nor
definable feeling, but a profusion of organic and tactile sensations
(cf. pp. 56, 59, 61, 115–16) or else elemental images (cf. pp.
59, 61, 114, 115). It is through these sensations and images that
the reader gradually discovers Dewey Dell's anxieties, anxieties
which she is unable to translate into words.

This incapacity to extricate oneself from the chaos of lived
experience is found again in young Vardaman. Not that his monologues are always pure confusion. He sometimes recounts what
he is doing very clearly: "Then I begin to run. I run toward the
back and come to the edge of the porch and stop. Then I begin to
cry" (p. 52). Snatches of narrative like this have the "flat" and
objective quality which is characteristic of the idiot Benjy's monologue in *The Sound and the Fury:* a series of gestures suggested
by simple words and sentences, all based on the same paratactic
pattern, and adding together without ever adding up. But this
appearance of objectivity is warped repeatedly by the strange
equation Vardaman makes between his dead mother and a fish.
His is the fluid prelogical world of a child in which all metamor-
phoses are possible. And like Dewey Dell's desire for an abortion, this *idée fixe* in Vardaman's mind linking mother and fish
returns again and again as a leitmotif in his monologues, his
whole perception of reality revolving around this metaphor.

Thus section 35 (pp. 143–44), where Vardaman gives his
own version of the river scene, is certainly a fragment of the narrative, but disrupted by the violent emotion which overcomes the
child when he sees the coffin swallowed up by the water. Until the
relationship between outside reality (coffin, water) and private
fantasy (mother, fish) has been recognized by the reader, the
monologue hardly makes sense. For it is the panic caused by the
perception of this analogy which erupts into the narrative and

causes it to disintegrate. Corresponding to the utter confusion in Vardaman's mind here is a breakdown of language of which the most obvious signs are irregularities in spelling ("darl" for "Darl"), the absence of punctuation (except in the last five lines), and the dislocation of syntax. A riot of words dash and crash into each other, disappear and reappear; sentences are started and lost, repeated and mixed up, unable to find their rightful place or order. Reference to reality is certainly still present; in the midst of this whirling confusion we still perceive the echo of words spoken, the reflection of things seen, but so jumbled and scattered that their sequential logic escapes us altogether. The narrative value of such a section is almost nil; the discourse itself is reduced to frenzied verbal gesticulation, to stammering punctuated by shouts ("hollering"). Nothing is left but the dizzy anguish of a consciousness caught up in the event.

Each point of view, then, achieves its unity through its underlying linguistic and psychological configuration; each narrator may be identified by his voice (or by what linguists would call his idiolect). True, another voice sometimes interrupts that of the character. Thus in one of the Vardaman sections there is the lavish description of a horse (p. 55). Clearly this piece of rhetoric bears no relation to the inchoate language of a child; the voice speaking here is none other than the author's. Faulkner, contrary to what one might have expected, does not restrict himself to colloquial realism. It is not unusual for his characters to start thinking and speaking beyond their means, to express themselves in a style incompatible with their level of consciousness as well as with their social status. Is the novelist to be censured for these fits of ventriloquy? Do they not threaten to destroy the coherence of the different points of view? In fact, the author's voice *augments* those of the narrators more than it obliterates them. No doubt Darl's speculations on being and nothingness far exceed the capacity for abstraction and reasoning of an uneducated young Mississippi farmer, but they convey eloquently the character's secret obsessions, bringing into the light of language all the unspoken obscurity seething within his tortured mind.

It is true that by probing the innermost thoughts in this way, there is a risk of reviving the absolute viewpoint of the traditional novel, but the author's self-effacement in *As I Lay Dying* is in any case only a clever pretense. Giving up, apparently, the privilege of the novelist-God, Faulkner most often hides behind his characters, and pretends to listen to them and let them tell the tale in his stead. Yet how could anyone without uncommon powers of divination transport himself into the minds of fifteen different narrators? Is the extreme multiplicity of points of view not, in the end, omniscience in disguise?[12] The technique used in *As I Lay Dying* conceals the novelist so that he can operate more freely in the wings. It is by no means a guarantee of realism; it is simply a creative method suited to the writer's purpose. Far from encroaching upon the novelist's prerogatives, it makes him all-powerful by making him invisible.

5

The Characters

CHARACTERIZATION

IN HIS INTERVIEWS Faulkner often repeated that his aim was to create "flesh-and-blood people that will stand up and cast a shadow."[1] However modern his approach to fiction, he never considered "characters" as outmoded accessories unworthy of his talent. Like Balzac and the other great demiurge novelists of the nineteenth century, Faulkner, in his own fashion, competed with God the Father,[2] attempting to make the world anew in his own image and peopling it with the creatures of his imagination. His novels, to be sure, are something more than stories in which memorable characters live and move, but they are that too. *As I Lay Dying* is both the tale of an adventure and the portrait of a family. Yet one must immediately add that although Faulkner does not scorn the old novelistic virtues and occasionally resorts to proven procedures, his art always avoids the facile and ultimately owes little to convention. The character remains, but free from the limitations of realistic description as well as from the artifices of psychological dissection.

In order to see better how characterization is effected in this novel, it is necessary to return to the interior monologue and to reconsider its significance as an instrument of psychological revelation. In *As I Lay Dying,* at the same time as being face, body,

attitude, or action, the character comes to life through his inner
speech. He exists in the silent discourse addressed to no one but
himself, and which at first one would not be able to ascribe to a
subject were it not for the name preceding it. In the monologue,
the character thus grows gradually from the inside. Not *seen* from
without but *heard* from within, he cannot be identified at once.
Transported without warning into the secret recesses of his mind,
where his most intimate thoughts, his most carefully hidden desires and obsessions are avowed, the reader at first gains little
knowledge from his closeness to the character; in fact he is too
close to discern his contours and too unfamiliar with the workings
of his mind to interpret them correctly. Yet, though we cannot see
the monologuing character, we see the world through his eyes and
temporarily share the way he responds to it. And after several
immersions in his stream of consciousness, we manage at last to
link this vision to an eye, this speech to a voice. Then we can stand
back and identify the character as a person.

The interior monologue provides access behind the scenes to
the closed and private world of obsessions and fantasies, but in
As I Lay Dying, as we have already noted, it never ceases to be a
mirror of the outside world and at the same time to react like a
seismograph to all its stimuli. Furthermore, we should not forget
that each monologue takes its place in a polyphonic ensemble. The
multiplicity of voices and eyes and the even greater multiplicity of
relationships established between them make each character in the
novel subject and object in turn: the focal point of perception in
one section is simply a perceived image in the next. The "I" of the
interior monologue tends to dissolve in the movement which carries it along; it suggests a presence rather than a person. But as
soon as, through someone else's eyes, this "I" becomes a "he," the
character assumes shape and substance and is invested with a character's attributes and prerogatives. The character is "I" as discovered by another and seen from without: smooth, hard, compact

as wood or stone. It is precisely in this way that Jewel appears to Darl in the opening section (p. 4). Wooden eyes, wooden face, wooden body, Jewel is what Darl is not and what he would like to be; he is the image of that impregnable fullness his own void envies. Jewel is to Darl what the "he" is to the "I" and it is certainly not by chance that Darl is most often presented in the first person, whereas Jewel remains almost throughout the novel a figure seen from outside.

This ever reversible and never transcended "I"-"he" relationship—a relationship dramatized by the antagonism between Darl and Jewel and whose tragic potential is indicated by Darl's ultimate madness (pp. 243–44)—confers a new status on the character by making it relative. What is more, its implementation in *As I Lay Dying,* with its continual reversals, allows the author once again to kill two birds with one stone: from the rich profusion of the interior monologue, the character derives his "depth"; from the circling fire of eyes he is exposed to, he acquires a parallel existence as an object which may be described at will. Thanks to this double perspective, each character is identified by his physical features, his gestures and actions, all the outward signs which manifest the particular mode of his behavior, as much as by the inflections of his inner voice. But there is nothing here which resembles the full-length portraits one finds in traditional fiction. Description is almost always done by the occasional brushstroke, and only rarely does it interrupt the flow of the narrative. And it goes without saying that it has no pretensions to absolute objectivity, since each character is necessarily seen and described by someone else.

Like a hall of mirrors, this interplay of subjectivities multiplies reflections and ambiguities, creates contrasts and misunderstandings, and never ceases to puzzle the reader. Between the way a character appears to himself and the way he appears to others there is an unbridgeable gap, and the switches from "I" to "he" and back force us to make constant readjustments. For a long time, for example, Addie appears only in the third person (she is almost silent during her agony and once a corpse becomes a mere object) and when at last, in section 40, we hear her speak in her own voice, the effect of surprise is complete. As for Dewey Dell, she long remains a diffuse presence, a faceless voice, and she is hard to recognize as the pretty little wildling described toward the end of the novel by Moseley and MacGowan. Several different profiles of the same character are thus sketched in. The intelligent, hypersensitive, and tormented Darl we know from his monologues contrasts strikingly with the strange lazy young man he is for the community and bears no relation whatever to the gentle and affectionate son described by Cora (p. 23). Likewise Addie appears in different lights according to whether she is evoked by her husband, her children, or the neighbors, or else confessing herself. Yet, contrary to what he does in *Absalom, Absalom!*, Faulkner ultimately makes little use of the Pirandellian mode to which his technique might lend itself. In *As I Lay Dying* the distortion which enters into the presentation of the characters results less from the crisscrossing of viewpoints than from the deliberate stylization imposed by the author.

Of each character he describes, in fact, Faulkner keeps only those traits he considers significant and jettisons the rest. What guides him in his descriptions is, as Jean-Jacques Mayoux remarks, "the search for expressiveness and superexpressiveness."[3] Hence the avalanches of epithets he heaps on the heroes' heads, epithets for the most part abstract, often grouped in pairs of opposites and reiterated throughout the novel:

In the lantern light his face is *calm, musing:* slowly he strokes his hands on his rain-coated thighs in a gesture *deliberate, final* and *composed.* [of Cash, p. 75]
Her face is *calm* and *sullen,* her eyes *brooding* and *alert.* [of Dewey Dell, p. 97]

Jewel looks at us again, his expression *sober* and *alert* and *sub-dued*. [p. 136]

Faces and gestures are not, strictly speaking, described. The expression alone counts, the meaning alone is specified. Most of the epithets refer to permanent traits rather than to transient moods; some of them are even attached to the characters like motifs: Cash is "composed" and "calculant," Dewey Dell "sullen" and "brooding," Jewel "furious." Yet it is also noteworthy that adjectives such as "alert" and "calm" are nearly interchangeable among most of the protagonists, characterizing then not what distinguishes one from another but the condition halfway between turbulence and rigidity which stamps them all.

What interests Faulkner is not therefore the body but, as Mayoux again notes, "the language of the body."[4] To translate this silent language the novelist uses an expressionist technique, both brutal and powerful: he simplifies the lines, thickens the features, flattens the contours, sacrificing the subtlety and nuance of the portrait to the suggestive vigor of the sketch. By way of example, consider the following snapshot of Vardaman at the moment when his mother is about to die: "Vardaman peers, with his round head and his eyes round and his mouth beginning to open" (p. 46). Nothing but rounds: it is as sketchy and as bluntly expressive as a child's drawing. Round head, eyes round, mouth open, Vardaman here loses all individuality to become an allegory of stupor. The same tendency toward extreme simplification may be seen in the way Faulkner uses colors. They are laid on thick and bright. Jewel's face is alternately red and green (pp. 91–92, 120), and Cash's, after the fording of the river where he was nearly drowned, is nothing but a patch of grey (pp. 148, 149, 197). Hurled on the canvas in vivid splashes, colors, just like shapes, are treated regardless of realism, and function first and foremost as signs.

In this endless search for the significant, Faulkner comes to grant a privileged place to the most expressive parts of the human body: the *hands* and the *eyes*. This is how he describes Addie's hands when she is dead:

> a curled, gnarled inertness; a spent yet alert quality from which weariness, exhaustion, travail has not yet departed, as though they doubted even yet the actuality of rest, guarding with horned and penurious alertness the cessation which they know cannot last. [p. 50]

Even in death, Addie's hands look strangely alive; their immobility appears to be merely provisional, as if they were to resume activity at any moment. A whole lifetime of hard work is summed up in these gnarled and alert hands. By contrast, Anse's hands, described on the following page (p. 51), are mere clumsy claws; useless in the simplest job (Anse cannot even manage to smooth a blanket!), they have apparently no other function than to let their owner scratch his head or rub his knee.

Actions, gestures, attitudes, all the movements of the body thus constitute a most revealing pantomime. If Darl's being is totally absorbed into sight and (inner) speech, that of most of the other Bundrens reveals itself through their ways of acting. Jewel is by turns fury and immobility; Cash is the slow, sure, precise gestures of a craftsman whom nothing can distract from his task, and Dewey Dell, when she waves her fan near the death-bed (pp. 8, 31, 42, 47) or when she wipes Cash's face with the hem of her dress (pp. 149, 155) spontaneously adopts a woman's ritual gestures at a time of suffering and death.

Yet the language of the eyes obviously engages Faulkner's interest more than any other. It is in their look that the characters' secret lives are concentrated, their hopes and anxieties disclosed, and it is primarily through their eyes that they communicate with one another. In their descriptions of Addie in her death throes, Darl, Cora, and Doctor Peabody all return continually to her eyes, in which the dying embers of her consciousness and energy are gathered in a final flicker:

Her eyes are like two candles when you watch them gutter down
into the sockets of iron candle-sticks. [p. 8]
Her eyes look like lamps blaring up just before the oil is gone.
[p. 44]
her eyes, the life of them suddenly rushing upon them; the two
flames glare up for a steady instant. [p. 47]

Everything happens as if the eyes had taken over from the other
senses. Addie's eyes listen:

as if her eyes alone are listening to the irrevocable cessation of his
voice. [p. 46]

They touch and push with terrific force:

She looks at us. Only her eyes seem to move. It's like they touch us,
not with sight or sense, but like a stream from a hose touches you.
. . . [p. 43]

If Faulkner seldom describes faces, his fascination with eyes
never abates, and in *As I Lay Dying* the eyes of the main characters are repeatedly described. Anse's eyes "look like pieces of
burnt-out cinder, fixed in his face, looking out over the land"
(pp. 30–31). Dewey Dell's are now sullenly bovine, now fiercely
aggressive: "If her eyes had a been pistols," Samson remarks, "I
wouldn't be talking now. I be dog if they didn't blaze at me" (pp.
108–109). Vardaman's are "round and black in the middle like
when you throw a light in an owl's face" (p. 66), and Jewel's
"look like pale wood in his high-blooded face" (p. 17). Lastly,
there are Darl's eyes, "them queer eyes of hisn that makes folks
talk" (p. 119). Transcending space and flesh, their capacity for
sight seems unlimited: "his eyes gone further than the food and
the lamp, full of the land dug out of his skull and the holes filled
with distance beyond the land" (pp. 25–26). Half *voyeur*, half
voyant, Darl is nothing but his look, and this look probes people's
hearts as easily as it covers distances: "It's like he had got into the
inside of you, someway. Like somehow you was looking at your-

self and your doings outen his eyes" (p. 119). No secret escapes him. Before his eyes, Dewey Dell feels stark naked:

> The land runs out of Darl's eyes; they swim to pin-points. They begin at my feet and rise along my body to my face, and then my dress is gone: I sit naked on the seat above the unhurrying mules, above the travail. [p. 115]

Throughout their journey the Bundrens constantly eye and spy on one another. The whole complex web of their conflicting relationships can be traced in the play of their looks. Ever on the qui vive, ever "alert," their eyes both reflect their vigilance and betray their passions. In their exposed frailty, they are flesh at its most vulnerable, testifying to that essential "nakedness" which is at the core of man's condition. As watchful sentinels of the mind, on the other hand, they assume a crucial role in each character's strategy of self-defense. A look can become a weapon of formidable power; it can lay bodies and souls bare, cutting to the quick, probing into the best-kept secrets. Yet if it is most often an instrument of defense or aggression, it can also be a privileged means of understanding and communication. When mutual suspicion disappears for a moment, the exchange of looks can be a sharing of some old forgotten terror, a fusing of two minds in an experience beyond words:

> he and I look at one another with long probing looks, looks that plunge unimpeded through one another's eyes and into the ultimate secret place where for an instant Cash and Darl crouch flagrant and unabashed in all the old terror and the old foreboding, alert and secret and without shame. [p. 135]

In reading the numerous descriptions of eyes in this novel, one cannot fail to be struck, too, by the need the author feels to complete and illuminate them with comparisons. Two examples have already been mentioned: Anse's cinder eyes and Jewel's wooden ones. Many others may be found. In the case of Jewel alone, his eyes are compared not only to wood, but to marbles (p.

94), pieces of a broken plate (p. 120), bleached chips (p. 138), "spots of white paper pasted on a high small football" (p. 203), and to two small torches (p. 208). We note here again Faulkner's taste for analogy and, more especially, his tendency to draw the animate towards the inanimate, to congeal human faces and bodies into inert objects. Thus Jewel is very frequently associated with "wood" and "wooden" (pp. 4, 17, 18, 89, 97, 102, 116, 173, 198, 221); the color of his eyes, his fixed stare, his stiff bearing, everything about him conjures up the idea of wood, everything, that is, except his legs, whose mobility has something incongruous and almost mechanical about it by contrast. Anse too seems roughhewn from wood (pp. 73–74, 156), and Peabody likens Addie on her deathbed to "a bundle of rotten sticks" (p. 43).

Apart from these material analogies there are many associations between the characters and the animal world. Jewel is at one with his horse and gallops through the novel like a demented centaur, Vardaman is linked with the image of the fish as if it were his totem, and Dewey Dell's bovine, ruminant femininity calls in two scenes for the actual presence of a cow (pp. 59–61, 241). But the most animalized of all the characters is undoubtedly Anse. His wife compares him to "a tall bird" (p. 162), Peabody refers to him as "a dipped rooster" (p. 43), and in one of Darl's sections his humped silhouette suggests the image of an owl (p. 48). And as if these ornithological references were not sufficient, Anse is also likened to a dog (pp. 17, 163), a bull (pp. 59, 69), and a horse (p. 117).

Finally one might mention again the significant links with sculpture and painting. Addie's face when she is dead is like "a casting of fading bronze" (p. 50). Jewel and his horse are "like two figures carved for a tableau savage in the sun" (p. 12); in the fire scene Jewel is twice described as a flat figure cut from tin (pp. 208, 211), and when he fights Gillespie, the two men, standing out against the red glare of the fire, evoke "figures in a

Greek frieze" (p. 211). Likewise Cash is seen as a painted figure; when he is hauled dripping from his near-drowning, his hair is stuck to his forehead "as though done with a paint-brush" (p. 149; see also p. 84). In these tableau scenes, the character, flattened, reduced to a surface or fixed as a statue (a procedure which may be compared to the "still" effect used in the French "new novel"), suddenly becomes unreal, like a pure image stopped in midflight, and reenters the space he had left only by means of an illusion: representational space.

We are a long way here from the credible, lifelike characters of realistic convention. Faulkner departs from this convention both by reduction to the grotesque and by mythical amplification. The reifying similes and expressionistic procedures just examined dehumanize the characters, and insofar as this dehumanization is both comic and disquieting in its effects, it inevitably veers toward the grotesque. In *As I Lay Dying* the element of the grotesque is obvious enough, but its importance varies with the character. Addie escapes it almost entirely; Darl has the merest brush with it; Jewel and Cash, on the other hand, often appear as clownish figures. As for Anse, he is unquestionably the great comic creation of the novel. Of all the characters, he is the most minutely described, the one whose portrait is most carefully detailed (pp. 16, 17, 30–31, 48–49, 72–74, 81). He also comes closest to a stock character; among the protagonists of the novel he is the most static and, in E. M. Forster's sense, the "flattest."[5] Throughout the novel he is the same unkempt and toothless gangling lout. His whole being is limited to a number of heavily scored features, whose recurrence underlines their unalterable stability: Anse's motivation is reduced to an *idée fixe* ("Now I can get them teeth"), and his appearances in the book are heralded by the return of the same ludicrous silhouette, the repetition of the same gestures (scratching his head, rubbing his knees), the same dumb show (blinking, "mumbling his mouth") and the same sententious and whining phrases. Anse is an odd body, a "humour," a pure caricature in the Dickensian tradition and in the popular humorous vein of the old Southwest,[6] hacked out by the "savage caricaturist" (pp. 73–74) who is none other than Faulkner himself.

The techniques used by the novelist are nonetheless susceptible of producing other effects. Instead of belittling the character, reducing him to the insignificance of a puppet, they can also serve to heighten and enlarge him. Even Anse, shabby as he is, ceases to be a comic type from time to time, suddenly achieving tragic stature; the passage from one to the other can occur within the space of a single sentence:

> Pa lifts his face, slack-mouthed, the wet black rim of snuff plastered close along the base of his gums; from behind his slack-faced astonishment he muses as though from beyond time, upon the ultimate outrage. [p. 72]

From a realism almost repellent in its detail, one swings suddenly (after "gums") into the great Faulknerian abstractions: here is Anse transported beyond time, and the storm gathering on the horizon, the rain which has begun to pour down become symbols of the "ultimate outrage," against which the farmer can and could pit nothing but the resigned innocence of his inexhaustible astonishment. Once the comic mask has fallen, Faulkner's man remains with his stupor before the scandal of his fate.

If Anse, a farcical latter-day Job, briefly appears here in a tragic light, Jewel draws us many a time into the violent and fabulous world of the epic. Critics have seen in him an avatar of Dionysus,[7] linked his adventures with those of Bellerophon and Pegasus, the winged horse, or compared his exploits to the labors of Hercules.[8] Jewel indeed evokes the world of pure qualities and forces in which the great heroes of mythology move. In the ritual fire-dance at the end of section 3 (p. 12), he is fused, exalted, annihilated with his horse in a prodigious whirl of light, intensity, movement, and power. And when, after his last feat, Jewel emerges from the blazing barn carrying the coffin like a trophy saved from the flames, his body silhouetted against the fire becomes the magnified image of a conquering hero.

Among the female characters this mythical transfiguration is equally apparent. While retaining identity as individualized characters, Dewey Dell and Addie both suggest the brooding presence of the Eternal Feminine. Like many of Faulkner's heroines, Dewey Dell—whose very name is heavily symbolic—is a maternal Eve at one with the immemorial earth: "I feel like a wet seed wild in the hot blind earth" (p. 61). By the vegetable image associating the woman's pregnancy with the germination of the seed, Faulkner points once again to the intimate relationship between feminine sexuality and earthly fecundity. Like Lena Grove (*Light in August*), Eula Varner (*The Hamlet*), or the anonymous woman in "Old Man" (*The Wild Palms*), Dewey Dell belongs to Faulkner's mammalian fertility symbols; she is *natura naturans,* and the life forces quickening her belly are no different from those that speed the harvest. So Darl, in a "metaphysical" conceit worthy of Donne, compares his sister's leg to Archimedes' lever that moves the world:

> her leg coming long beneath the tightening dress: that lever which moves the world; one of that caliper which measures the length and breadth of life. [pp. 97–98]

Further on, the same correspondence between microcosm and macrocosm arises in one of the strangest visions in the whole book:

> Squatting, Dewey Dell's wet dress shapes for the dead eyes of three blind men those mammalian ludicrosities which are the horizons and the valleys of the earth. [p. 156]

Addie is likewise transformed into an archetypal figure. But the earth to which she is attached first and foremost is the "ultimate earth," the shadowy kingdom of the dead, not the womb of the living. When Cash looks at her for the last time, he sees her face "fading into the dusk as though darkness were a precursor of the ultimate earth" (p. 49). Addie is no living seed but dug up roots (p. 15) or rotten wood (p. 43). Yet in her monologue these images of death, recalled at the beginning by the reference to "damp and rotting leaves" (p. 161) and echoed by her father's haunting reflections on the ineluctability of death (p. 161, 165, 167), are counterbalanced by Addie's portrayal of herself in the role of the life-giving earth mother. Her passionate identification with the elemental powers of the earth is suggested throughout her soliloquy. After becoming a mother, she listens in the dark to "the land that [is] now [her] blood and flesh" (p. 165). When she gives birth to Cash, she feels as if she were everyone's mother, and even Anse becomes her potential child: "I would think that if he were to wake and cry, I would suckle him, too" (p. 164). Addie projects her motherhood on a cosmic scale:

My children were of me alone, of the wild blood boiling along the earth, of me and of all that lived; of none and of all. [p. 167]

Addie is thus equated with Genitrix, the *Magna Mater* of archaic religions. But while it may be tempting to compare Addie and Dewey Dell to Demeter and Persephone,[9] or to other fertility goddesses, it must also be recognized that all this symbolism tends to be reversed and that once more irony prevails. Unlike Lena Grove, Dewey Dell stubbornly refuses maternity and thinks only of having an abortion. As for Addie, she is indeed a mother figure, but she embodies motherhood associated with death rather than life, hatred rather than love. In *As I Lay Dying* it is the "wicked mother" who eventually predominates. The children Addie bore were not only unloved or ill loved in her lifetime; she seems to be hounding them even after her death by all the ordeals she inflicts upon them, and it almost looks as if she were reaching out from beyond time to drag them after her into the nether world. In her unrelenting vindictiveness, she is a cruel stepmother rather than a mother, Hecate or Medea rather than the all-loving Demeter.

Dehumanized or superhuman, hurled into the sky of myth or reduced to the condition of beasts or mere things, the Faulknerian character, in all his shapes and guises, proves extraordinarily malleable. The novelist's imagination grips him, stretches or squashes him, fattens or flattens him; it distorts and disfigures him at will. But despite all this ill treatment, he manages to exist within the space of the book and cast his shadow there as Faulkner intended. The shadow may be disproportionately large or fantastically deformed, but it is nonetheless the living likeness of a human shadow.

THE BUNDREN FAMILY

LIKE most of Faulkner's novels, *As I Lay Dying* is a family chronicle. But the Bundrens' story is more easily followed than that of the Sartorises, the Compsons, the Sutpens, or the McCaslins. The Bundrens are not part of any Southern dynasty, have no famous ancestor to be proud or ashamed of (the only character from the past who figures in the book is Addie's father), and no tradition, no legacy has been entrusted to them. History is no dimension of their lives and the family pattern is here at its simplest: father, mother, sons, and daughter form the archetypal kernel from which the novel grows.

If *As I Lay Dying* differs from Faulkner's other novels by its lack of genealogical complications, the family presented in the book nonetheless bears some striking similarities to those he evokes elsewhere. First in its composition: the Bundrens have four sons and one daughter; in *The Sound and the Fury* likewise there are several boys and one girl,[10] and in yet other novels one finds a single sister in the midst of "a roaring gang of menfolks."[11] It is curious to note in this respect that Faulkner himself had three brothers and no sister, and that in creating the character of Caddy Compson he had intended, on his own admission, to make up for the absence of a real sister by giving himself an imaginary one.[12]

Another, more essential, feature which links the Bundrens to the other Faulkner families is their division. In *As I Lay Dying* the family sticks together as long as its survival is at stake; it defends itself like a threatened organism against all outside dangers, and so triumphs over all the obstacles set in its path on the journey to Jefferson. But this clannish solidarity in the face of danger is no victory over individual isolation; it does not prevent each one remaining walled in by solitude, and serves only to mask the drama smoldering within the family. As Calvin Bedient puts it, the family is "a terrible and frustrating unit of interlocking solitudes, atomic in structure like a molecule."[13] Family relationships are all marked by conflict, and this novel presents almost the whole range of possible tensions. Faulkner sets against each other husband and wife (Anse/Addie), mother and son (Addie/Darl), father and daughter (Anse/Dewey Dell), brother and brother (Darl/Jewel), and brother and sister (Darl/Dewey Dell). One antagonism alone is not explicitly evoked—we shall soon try to see why—that between father and son. Finally, like *The Sound and the Fury* and *Absalom, Absalom!*, *As I Lay Dying* lets it be understood that at the root of the children's wretchedness are the sins of the parents.

Addie

The nub of all the tensions generated within the Bundren family is Addie, in her dual role as wife and mother. Herself a creature of conflict, "a lonely woman, lonely with her pride" (p. 21), haunted by death and impatient to live, she has never been able to reconcile her contradictory needs; her whole existence has been torn between the desperate desire to live and communicate, to reach "the burning heart of life,"[14] and the equally imperious wish to preserve her solitude and integrity as an individual. The presence within Addie of these conflicting aspirations, this double movement of acquiescence and refusal, surrender and withdrawal, is enough to set her apart from the general run of mother figures one finds in Faulkner. Whereas Lena Grove is from the outset at one with the rhythms of the earth, this fusion with the world is perhaps only wishful thinking for Addie. It is true that the picture of herself she projects in her monologue is that of an earth mother. But can we really take *her word* for it?

Addie herself tells us to beware of words. Why then should we trust hers? Is there not something suspect in her strident rhetoric, and is her monologue not, in the end, an admission of failure? In fact her eloquence is a man's eloquence, just as her passion is masculine; it is the fire of a chimerical imagination rather than the warmth of a simple heart. Addie has been compared with Hester Prynne;[15] features have been found in common with D.H. Lawrence's heroines. Although the juxtaposition may seem surprising, she has even deeper affinities perhaps with Emma Bovary, at least as Baudelaire saw her: "Imagination, supreme and tyrannical faculty, in place of the heart. . . . Sudden outbursts of action, speed of decision, mystical fusion of reason and passion. . . . Excessive taste for seduction and for domination. . . ."[16] These features are almost all found in Faulkner's heroine as much as in Flaubert's. Baudelaire saw in Madame Bovary a "bizarre androgyne," an "almost male" being who gives herself "in a quite masculine way to despicable fellows who are not her equals";[17] Addie gives herself, or rather *takes* in the same way (cf. p. 163: "So I took Anse"). Imagination, energy, impatience, pride, she has the virtues and the flaws that Faulkner attributes to his most virile heroes (to Thomas Sutpen for example). As Cleanth Brooks very shrewdly notes,[18] there is so to speak an inversion of roles in the novel: it is Anse, the husband, who has the inertia and endurance which the writer most often associates with his female characters; and it is Addie who embodies the crazy and ultimately destructive dream of man. Masculinized like Drusilla, egocentric like Mrs. Compson (but without her whining self-pity, which has been transferred to Anse), Addie also makes one think of Charlotte Rittenmeyer, another virile woman and another adulteress, whose exacerbated romanticism is strangely like her own.

The perverted "feminine principle" finds in Addie one of its most gripping portrayals. Yet she is not only a "wicked mother," she also becomes to some extent an image of paternity. Marked by the memory of her death-haunted father (as Quentin is by Mr. Compson's pessimism), Addie in her turn becomes a father figure to her children. Her relations with them are primarily relations of authority and domination, foreshadowed by the whippings she gave her pupils when she was a schoolmistress. Addie's sadism may be interpreted as a desperate attempt to conquer loneliness, but it is even more the desire to break into the intimacy of others, the wish to force them to reveal themselves through their pain and pay homage to their torturer. Violence answers Addie's thirst for reality; it is for her a shortcut to communication, a way to gain recognition of her self by others, yet there is no love in it, since it denies recognition of the other in his otherness and thus prevents true reciprocity.

This need for self-assertion, in its fundamental ambivalence,[19] has governed Addie's whole life. But it is paradoxically in and through death that her domineering will enjoys its surest —and also its most derisory—triumph. By demanding burial at Jefferson, by imposing on her family the daunting ordeals of the journey, Addie, for one last time, makes them obey her law. Dead, and transformed by death into an indestructible presence, she exercises even more absolute power, comparable to that of the great paternal or ancestral shades which one senses hovering over so many of Faulkner's novels, and which seem by their very remoteness to increase their hold over the living. The novelist

Addie

In the afternoon when school was out and the last one had left with his little dirty snuffly nose, instead of going home I would go back down the hill to the spring where I could be quiet and hate them. It would be quiet there then, with the water bubbling up and away and the sun slanting quiet in the trees and the quiet smell of damp and rotting leaves and new earth; especially in the early spring, for it was worst then.

I could just remember how my father used to say that the reason for living was to get ready to die. And when I would think that this seemed to be the only way I could get ready to die, I would hate my father for having even planted me. have to look at them, each with his and her secret and selfish thought, and blood strange to each other blood and strange to mine, and think that this seemed to be the only way I could get ready to die, I would hate my father for even having ever planted me. And so when they failed I would look forward to the time when they failed, so I could whip them. When the switch fell I could feel it upon my flesh; when it welted it was my blood that ran, and I would think with each blow of the switch: Now you are aware of me. Now I am something in your life, who have marked your blood with my own.

And so I took Anse. I would see him pass the school saw him pass the school house 3 or 4 times before I knew that he was going 4 miles out of his way to do it. I noticed then how he was beginning to hump — a tall man and young — so that he looked already like a tall bird hunched in the cold weather, on the wagon seat. He would pass the schoolhouse, the wagon creeping past, his head turning slow to look at the door of the schoolhouse, until the wagon passed on around the curve. One day I went to the door and stood there when he passed. When he saw me he looked quickly away and did not look back again.

In the early spring it was worst. Sometimes I thought that I could not bear it, lying in bed at night, with the wild geese going north and their honking coming out of the wild darkness, and during the day it would come on me so that I couldn't wait for the last one to go so I could go down to the spring. And so when I looked up that day and saw Anse standing there in his Sunday clothes, turning his hat round and round in his hands, I said:

"If you've got any womenfolks, why in the world don't they make you get your hair cut?"

In the afternoon when school was out and the last one had left with his little dirty snuffling nose, instead of going home I would go back down the hill to the spring where I could be quiet and hate them. It would be quiet there then, with the water bubbling up and in and the sun slanting quiet in the trees and the quiet smelling of damp and rotting leaves and new earth; especially in the early spring, for it was worst then.

I could just remember how my father used to say that the reason for living was to get ready to die. And when I would ~~think that this seemed to be the only way I could get ready to die. I would hate my father for having ever planted me.~~ have to look at them [day after day]*, each with his and her secret and selfish thot and blood strange to each other blood and strange to mine, and think that this seemed to be the only way I could get ready to die, I would hate my father for (ever) having ever planted me. And so ~~when they faulted~~ I would look forward to the time when they faulted, so I could whip them. When the switch fell I could feel it upon my flesh; when it welted it was my blood that ran, and I would think with each blow of the switch: Now you are aware of me. Now I am something in your life, who have marked your blood with my own.

And so I took Anse. I ~~would see him pass the school~~ saw him pass the school house 3 or 4 times before I learned that he was driving 4 miles out his way to do it. I noticed then how he was beginning to hump—a tall man and young—so that he looked already like a tall bird hunched in the cold weather, on the wagon seat. He would pass the school house, the wagon creaking slow, his head turning slow to look at the door of the school house, until the wagon passed on around the curve. One day I went to the door and stood there when he passed. When he saw me he looked quickly away and did not look back again.

In the early spring it was worst. Sometimes I thot that I could not bear it, lying in bed at night, with the wild geese going north and their honking coming out of the wild darkness, and during the day it would seem as tho I couldn't wait for the last one to be gone so I could go down to the spring. And so when I looked up that day and saw Anse standing there in his Sunday clothes, turning his hat round and round in his hands, I said:

"If you've got any womenfolks, why in the world don't they make you get your hair cut?"

* This phrase is written in the margin of the manuscript.

Transcript of the beginning of Addie's monologue (page 69 of the manuscript), *As I Lay Dying*, pp. 161–63.

thus endows Addie with the attributes of head of the clan and the virtues of the totem traditionally reserved for the male. She is at once a mother in flesh and a father in spirit. She is the matriarchal sovereign.

Anse

If Addie is queen bee, Anse is the drone. A weak husband[20] and an irresponsible father, he lives among his family as an impenitent parasite. Never working because, the story has it, the doctors have forbidden him to sweat (pp. 16–17), unloading all his work onto his sons and if necessary his neighbors, he detests the road, hates movement, and dreams placidly of the immobile existence of the trees (p. 35). But let there be no mistake: Anse's placidity is not as innocent as it appears at first. Indeed, there is scarcely a character in Faulkner so loaded with faults and vices. Anse is not only unbelievably lazy, he also proves himself in the course of the journey to be an accomplished hypocrite, playing to perfection the role of the grief-stricken widower (cf. p. 74: "a monstrous burlesque of all bereavement") and parading grand sentiments when all the time he is thinking of buying his false teeth and replacing Addie by another wife. An idle, wily, speechifying Tartuffe in Job's clothing, Anse hides under his clownish mask and helpless mien a massive and ruthless egoism. His inertia is no weakness; it is a force which he manipulates cleverly to achieve his own ends and, as Samson remarks (p. 108), once he's started, there's no stopping him. If he seems to have, up to a certain point, a sense of family honor (a feature overemphasized perhaps by critics), his feelings towards his wife and children are nil. Whether it is a question of Addie's illness or Cash's broken leg, their sufferings leave him indifferent and his avarice makes him wait till the last minute to call the doctor. And soon, behind the weak father appears the predatory father: enjoying the immunity which the dregs of his paternal authority allow him, Anse does not hesitate to swap Jewel's horse surreptitiously for a pair of mules, nor does he have the slightest scruple about stealing Cash's and Dewey Dell's meagre savings. The conversation he has with his daughter when he is about to take her ten dollars clearly shows what fierce determination lies hidden beneath his hollow rhetoric (sect. 58, pp. 245–46). For Cleanth Brooks, Anse is undoubtedly one of the gallery of Faulkner's monsters:

> Anse Bundren is one of Faulkner's most accomplished villains. He lacks the lethal power of a Popeye and the passionate intensity of a Percy Grimm, but the kind of force that he embodies has to be reckoned with. It is deceptively slight, as delicately flexible as a root tendril but, like the tendril, powerful enough to break a boulder. Anse resembles most nearly Flem Snopes—in his coolness, his sheer persistence, his merciless knowledge of other human beings and of how much they will put up with.[21]

Anse might indeed be one of the Snopeses. He has their callousness, their gnawing patience, and their ratlike talent for survival. But the verve, mischief, and outrageous humor with which Faulkner has drawn the character almost make us forget it.

Cash

Cash is the oldest of the Bundren children. With Jewel, he is Addie's favorite, and there is an understanding between him and his mother which does not require the use of words: "Cash did not need to say it to me nor I to him" (p. 164). His love for her is expressed by his meticulous ardor in the construction of the coffin; his hands and tools take the place of words for him and his whole morality is essentially based on work. Cash is a good carpenter, proud of his craft, hard working, conscientious, methodical to the point of mania. His is a world of figures and measurements, a craftsman's or a technician's world. His first monologue tells us nothing other than the thirteen carefully numbered reasons for making the coffin on the bevel (sect. 18, pp. 77–78), and in the following ones (sect. 22, p. 90; sect. 38,

p. 157) the fear that the coffin "wont balance" seems his one obsession. There is something both laughable and disturbing about this excess of professional conscience. Seeing Cash so thoroughly engrossed in the making and transportation of the coffin, one wonders if he has not forgotten what it contains. Unless the coffin is for him what the horse is for Jewel and the fish for Vardaman: the object of a transference.

It is true that in the first half of the novel Cash is presented as an essentially comic figure, and Faulkner misses no opportunity to make fun of his literal-mindedness (see, for example, the pre-posterous precision of his answer to Armstid's question about his first accident, on p. 83, and the revealing anecdote about his boy-hood recounted by Jewel, p. 14). But perhaps there is also, be-hind the stiffness and stolidity of this reasoning and reasonable character, a secret perplexity; maybe he too is not quite "on a balance." The picture drawn by Faulkner is in any case more subtle and more complex than it first appears. Cash is not only the absurdly busy carpenter we see at the beginning. Unimagina-tive as he may be, he lacks neither feeling nor intuition and, after Darl, it is he who seems to grasp most fully the meaning of the crisis his family is going through. Above all, Cash is the only one who shows understanding for Darl and his "madness"; he is even so close to him that he can read his thoughts (p. 137) and guess his intentions (p. 224). This silent communication be-tween the two older sons, particularly evident in the closing pages, is, however, suggested much earlier (p. 135). So it would seem excessive to speak of a profound transformation on Cash's part during the journey.[22] In fact the trials and sufferings he un-dergoes reveal his character more than they change it; they reveal it especially after he has broken his leg a second time: Cash accepts his lot without a murmur of complaint right to the end, as patient, as indefatigable and almost as comic in pain as he had been in his work.

This experience no doubt makes him all the more sensitive

to Darl's predicament. But the extent of his compassion must nonetheless be clearly plotted. Cash understands why his brother set fire to the barn and even approves his action to a certain degree (p. 223); he also knows how arbitrary the very notion of madness is (p. 228). Yet Cash accepts social norms, however debatable their principle may be in any absolute sense. His attitude toward madness is a corollary of his carpenter's morality. If he ultimately condemns Darl's burning of the barn, it is because it was a destructive gesture; for Cash, "nothing excuses setting fire to a man's barn and endangering his stock and destroying his property" (p. 223). His respect for other people's property stems directly from his respect for work: "there just aint nothing justifies the deliberate destruction of what a man has built with his own sweat and stored the fruit of his sweat into" (p. 228).

In the face of the world's absurdity and man's unreason, Cash, the good worker, *homo faber,* typifies a possible form of wisdom. It consists of resignation at the irremediable, at suffering and death, of submission to the established order and most of all of faith in work and in the creative resources of the individual. It is the wisdom of a builder and an owner, modest, reasonable, pragmatic, and prosaic; it requires humility and pride, courage and will, but dispenses with imagination altogether. Faulkner—who readily compared himself to a carpenter and who also loved a "neat job"—shows us with wry humor its virtues and its limitations.

Darl

The drama of Darl is rooted in what Faulkner calls elsewhere "the tragic complexity of motherless childhood."[23] Addie had not wanted her second son (p. 164); she has never accepted him, never loved him, and he waits in vain by her deathbed for her to recognize him at last, if only by a look, as her son (p. 24).[24] Darl has no mother: "I cannot love my mother because I have no mother" (p. 89). Does he hate her? The question is raised by his setting fire to the barn. Should his only action during the journey be explained by his desire to avenge himself on Addie? Or by his wish to thwart Jewel? Or is it, as Cash would have it, the reflex of common decency? These are all plausible hypotheses to which a further one might be added: could his act not be interpreted symbolically, as a last and desperate attempt to take possession of his mother?[25] What is certain is that the relationship between Darl and Addie is, if anything, destructive and that its utterly negative character is the main cause of Darl's incapacity to find his place in the chain of being.

With the other members of the family, Darl's relations are not all as negative. A long-standing complicity unites him to Cash, and with young Vardaman a different type of understanding is achieved through the affinity of madness and childhood and through a common search for identity. With Dewey Dell and Jewel, on the other hand, Darl's relations are strained, and their hatred for him explodes with savage violence at the end of the journey (pp. 226–27). Dewey Dell fiercely resents his having caught her with Lafe and his knowing the secret of her pregnancy. Confused and ambiguous, the relationship between Darl and Dewey Dell is like a vague reflection of the incestuous love of Quentin for his sister Caddy in *The Sound and the Fury*. But unlike Quentin, Darl, although a *voyeur* like him, is not jealous of his sister's lovers and her honor scarcely matters to him. His jealousy is directed at Jewel, the favorite son. It is resentful jealousy that lies behind the cruelty of the questions he needles him with ("Do you know she is going to die, Jewel?" "Your mother was a horse, but who was your father, Jewel?" Cf. pp. 38, 39, 51, 88, 202, 203) and that prompts his maneuver to prevent him from being present at his mother's death. It is fascinated jealousy above all, as is evident from the enormous importance Jewel is given in his monologues. "Jewel and I . . . ," so starts Darl's first section, and of the eighteen others attributed to him, ten open similarly with a reference to the resented and envied brother (cf. sect. 5, 10, 21, 23, 25, 27, 32, 42, 48, 50). Even when Jewel is not within sight, Darl's clairvoyant eye follows him at a distance, scrutinizing his every action with unflagging attention (cf. the italicized passages in sect. 3 and 42).

Why this fascination? Darl is entranced by Jewel as Sartre's *pour-soi* is by *en-soi*. Jewel *is,* and all the more so since he is unaware of it: "Jewel knows he is, because he does not know that he does not know whether he is or not" (p. 76). Whereas Darl not only doubts his identity, he doubts his very existence: "I dont know what I am, I dont know if I am or not" (p. 76). Deprived of all lineage, unloved and rootless, nobody's son, Darl is the merest fluid gesture of a being. His affliction is the affliction of consciousness, powerless to bring itself into focus, incapable of organizing and gathering itself around a fixed center, frightened by its own emptiness. Darl has no other shelter than words; estranged from reality and from himself, he is forever doomed to exile. "This world is not his world; this life his life," Cash says (p. 250). And as Darl has no home, here or elsewhere is all the same to him. Hence his plural self or, to borrow one of his own phrases, his "perverse ubiquity" (p. 51). His clairvoyance springs from his very weakness; it is a side effect of his ontological deficiency. Without anything to ballast or contain it, his mind can range freely and identify with any other mind it encounters on its way. Darl can become anyone because he is nothing himself.

What makes him a tragic figure is that he is intensely and painfully aware of his predicament. Jewel does not know that he *is;* Darl knows that he *is not* and suffers from the knowledge of his nonexistence. No one is more vulnerable than he, no one more exposed in his isolation and his nakedness. Having no identity to moor him in existence, no stable solid self to give him weight and balance, Darl lives in a world itself corroded by unreality and impermanence, a world on the verge of chaos and extinction (cf. pp. 196–97). And almost everywhere in his monologues we sense his obsession with nothingness, with dissolution, with the irresistible flux of time—an obsession which is both terror and temptation: "If you could just ravel out into time. That would be nice. It would be nice if you could just ravel out into time" (p. 198).

Whether Darl is mad or not from the outset is a debatable question. If Faulkner is to be believed, "Darl was mad from the start."[26] Indeed, it does not take us long to discover how precarious his mental balance is, and though there is little to suggest plain insanity in the first monologues, they provide enough clues for the reader not to be too surprised by his ultimate breakdown. All the classic symptoms of schizophrenia are soon discernible: withdrawal from reality, loss of vital contact with others, disembodiment and splitting of self, obsession with identity, sense of isolation and deadness, armageddonism (the sense that "the end of the world is nigh" apparent in Darl's account of the river scene).[27] It is scarcely surprising therefore that, with the ordeals of the journey to help, he ends by succumbing to madness.

Yet Darl's madness is actually something other than a case for psychiatrists. It is distress and disorder certainly, but it is also knowledge and poetry; it is as much a breakthrough as a breakdown. Of all the characters in *As I Lay Dying,* it is surely this rustic Hamlet who has the closest affinities with his creator. Faulkner makes him his principal narrator and to some extent one of his *alter egos:* if Cash is an image of the craftsman-novelist, Darl represents the novelist-poet. Of the gifts it takes to be a creative novelist Darl possesses the most precious: the faculty of vision, the "negative capability," the power of speech. In a way Darl is Faulkner's portrait of the artist as a young madman. What is more, he is also one of those wounded heroes (literally or figuratively) who appear so often in Faulkner's early novels: Donald Mahon, Bayard Sartoris, Quentin Compson, Horace Benbow. Behind all these dissimilar figures lies the same hidden malady, the same incapacity to live, the same terror of death. Through these other selves, the novelist attempted to pass from "I" to "he" (which becomes "I" again, but a fictional "I" in the monologues of Darl and Quentin); by keeping his invented characters at a distance, by withdrawing from their destinies, by making them where necessary die in his stead, he achieved the immunity of the creator. This difficult transfer from "I" to "he" (one has only to think of what this process of depersonalization meant for a writer like Kafka) is presented here in all its risky ambiguity by the closing scene of Darl's madness. Darl becomes the scapegoat, the *pharmakos,* not only of the Bundren family, but of the author himself. For the character in the novel, this madness means death, the final annihilation of self; for his creator, it represents the hazard of creation and perhaps the chance of its accomplishment.

Jewel

Jewel is everything Darl is not. While Darl is mere passive perception, Jewel is pure violence, and the fury which constantly grips him similarly distinguishes him from Cash. Both are no doubt men of action; Cash, the carpenter, however, in his methodical devotion to work, is essentially a builder, a civilizing hero, whereas Jewel, in his untamed energy and utter recklessness, rather suggests the dash and daring of some barbarian conqueror. He never acts in order to build but for acting's sake: "Just so we do something," he says at the time of the river crossing (p. 139). For Jewel passion and action are everything, and he feels no need for thought to mediate between them. As can be seen from the only section given to him, his inner world is a welter of violent emotions; action, any action, seems to be the only release he can find from their pent-up turbulence. Jewel has often been compared to the heroes and demigods of classical mythology; with his tall lean figure, his long hair, his pale eyes and intractable gait, he would not be at all out of place in that modern

American epic, the Western. Inarticulate, unreflective, aggressively masculine, Jewel has the brutal simplicity of the epic hero. He is a force, driving and driven, and by this token becomes the mainspring of action in the novel.

As a character, Jewel occupies a very special place in the Bundren family. More markedly than his sister and brothers, he defines himself first of all in relation to Addie. Yet, having been conceived in adultery, he is to some extent an outsider to the family and feels like one, although he hardly suspects his extramarital origin. Just as Darl has no mother, Jewel, the illegitimate offspring of Addie and preacher Whitfield, has no father. In both cases one parent is missing, but while being motherless has tragic consequences for Darl, the absence of a father and the exclusive intimacy it allowed to develop with the mother seem on the contrary to have confirmed Jewel in his being and to have given him more vital strength than any of the other Bundren children. Jewel is Addie's favorite, the child of her sin and rebellion, the inheritor of her violence. In her own private and idolatrous version of Christianity, she has even allowed him to usurp God and has appointed him prophetically as her Savior: "He is my cross and he will be my salvation" (p. 180). In his childhood Jewel therefore had almost to excess what had been persistently denied to Darl. His mother brooded over him with fierce and tender love; "ma always whipped him and petted him more," Darl recounts (p. 17). Out of this passionate love Jewel's own grew in return, equally intense, equally ambivalent, equally possessive.

Jewel is attached to his wild horse in a surprisingly similar way. He cherishes it as his prize possession; he never leaves it, even sleeps with it, and permits no one except himself to take care of it. The horse becomes the object of his love and hate. Jewel brutalizes and caresses it in turn, and curses it, in Darl's words, with "obscene ferocity" (p. 12). With his usual shrewdness, Darl does not fail to identify the treasured animal as a mother surrogate: "Jewel's mother is a horse" (p. 95). This strange transference (parallel in some ways to Vardaman's equation of Addie with a fish) is obviously a defense mechanism indicative of the incestuous nature of Jewel's love for his mother. Like Quentin Compson's, his is in some measure a forbidden love, an impossible love the reverse of which is his hatred for the other members of the family. The fantasy which closes his single monologue leaves no doubt about the fierce intolerance of his feelings for Addie. Just as Quentin wanted to isolate Caddy "out of the loud world,"[28] Jewel would kill father and brother to be alone with his mother and so be assured forever of exclusive rights:

> It would just be me and her on a high hill and me rolling the rocks down the hill at their faces, picking them up and throwing them down the hill faces and teeth and all. . . . [p. 15]

Dewey Dell

Dewey Dell and Vardaman, the youngest, were mere exchange values in Addie's moral accountancy, and they lacked motherly love just as Darl did. Dewey Dell was the child Addie gave her husband to "negative" Jewel, Vardaman the one to replace Cash, "the child [she] had robbed him of" (p. 168). Their mother's death throws them both into deep anguish; because they are the youngest—Dewey Dell is just out of adolescence and Vardaman is still a child—it strikes them more cruelly and leaves them completely at a loss. Their pathetic confusion expresses itself in their attitudes and gestures at the moment of Addie's death; with Vardaman, it is dumb stupor:

> From behind Pa's leg Vardaman peers, his mouth full open and all color draining from his face into his mouth, as though he has by some means fleshed his own teeth in himself, sucking. He begins to move slowly backward from the bed, his eyes round, his pale face fading into the dusk like a piece of paper pasted on a failing wall, and so out of the door. [p. 48]

With Dewey Dell, it is first loud wailing ("she begins to keen," p. 47), then violent gesticulation:

> she flings herself across Addie Bundren's knees, clutching her, shaking her with the furious strength of the young before sprawling suddenly across the handful of rotten bones that Addie Bundren left, jarring the whole bed into a chattering sibilance of mattress shucks, her arms outflung and the fan in one hand still beating with expiring breath into the quilt. [pp. 47–48]

It is therefore untrue to say as some critics have[29] that Dewey Dell is hardly affected by her mother's death. On the contrary, she feels it all the more intensely as it occurs at a time when she more than ever needs Addie. In whom could she confide her secret if not in her mother? Dewey Dell feels doubly betrayed, doubly deserted. Lafe seduced her and left her. Pregnant, she discovers, as Addie had at Cash's birth, her destiny as begetter; like her mother, she is snatched from her solitude only to be thrown back to it. And now her "aloneness" is made all the more irremediable by the death of the only person who could (or so she thinks) have understood and relieved her distress. The drama of Dewey Dell is that of an initiation which fails because it is premature. Everything—her first sexual experience, her pregnancy, her mother's death—everything comes to her too soon. Time, life, death, everything goes too quickly:

> I heard that my mother is dead. I wish I had time to let her die. I wish I had time to wish I had. It is because in the wild and outraged earth too soon too soon too soon. It's not that I wouldn't and will not it's that it is too soon too soon too soon. [p. 114]

Dewey Dell has no grip on events. She is caught up in them without having time to live them, think them, make them her own experience. She feels abandoned, defenseless, to dark forces which make her their instrument and plaything. Her *idée fixe,* the abortion, is primarily a protest against what happens to her, a revolt against the embryonic life developing within her and doing violence to her body. If only Doctor Peabody wanted to help her get rid of it, she would regain possession of her integrity: "Then I could be all right alone" (p. 57). Like Darl, Dewey Dell is obsessed by the problem of her identity. But the obsession—confirmed by the nightmare she had as a child (pp. 115–16)—has other causes in her. Her consciousness, unlike Darl's, is not dissociated from her body, but becomes ensnared and lost in it. The image Dewey Dell paints of herself is that of a "little tub of guts," and her whole universe is one mass of viscera (p. 56). Hers is a world trapped in flesh, an almost mindless world of sensory contacts and blind tropisms; her monologues drag us into a muggy limbo where life and death are inextricably tangled. Naked flesh, warm breath, dampness, darkness, all the images and sensations associated with Dewey Dell are organic, sexual, or cosmic. In *Ulysses,* Joyce had made Molly Bloom's sex talk. Here it is seemingly Dewey Dell's body which speaks. Yet a voice is heard at times above this confused murmur, one which is not simply the body, an anxious and faltering voice expressing at one and the same time the wish to be something other than flesh and the vanity of that wish, a voice which tells both of the terror and of the fascination of surrender:

> The dead air shapes the dead earth in the dead darkness, further away than seeing shapes the dead earth. It lies dead and warm upon me, touching me naked through my clothes. I said You dont know what worry is. I dont know what it is. I dont know whether I am worrying or not. Whether I can or not. I don't know whether I can cry or not. I dont know whether I have tried to or not. I feel like a wet seed wild in the hot blind earth. [p. 61]

Vardaman

Vardaman[30] is by no means the idiot some critics have wanted to make him.[31] He is a child (of unspecified age, but there are a number of references to his small size and one is led to suppose he is between six and eight) overwhelmed by his mother's death. He does not feel mere grief at it; for him death is something

[95

scandalous, monstrous, literally inconceivable, an event which throws him into the depths of anguish and bewilderment. In order to make Addie's death a part of his prelogical world—or rather to exorcise it from his mind—Vardaman performs a series of magical substitutions. His need to find its cause makes him first look for the culprit; he starts by placing the blame for his mother's death on Doctor Peabody, who arrived shortly before she died (pp. 52–53), and, unable to take it out on the doctor himself, he wreaks his revenge by thrashing the doctor's horses (pp. 53–54). In his mind it is enough for two events to be more or less simultaneous for there to be a cause-and-effect relationship between them; it is enough for them to be linked by some analogy to become virtually identical. That is how Vardaman manages to identify his mother with a fish. Some hours before her death he caught a big fish and splashed blood all over himself when cutting it up. Between these two occurrences spring up associations of puzzling complexity. Addie stopped being when the fish became not-fish. If the fish were still alive, so would his mother be, and since the death of the fish was a direct result of his own volition, it must be possible to backtrack, obliterate the occurrence, and then both mother and fish would be restored to him (pp. 63–64). To these pseudo-arguments based on analogy are added others which are just as wildly irrational. Vardaman also persuades himself that someone else has been substituted for Addie in the deathbed and that his mother has simply gone on a journey: "It was not her. I was there, looking. I saw. I thought it was her, but it was not. It was not my mother. She went away when the other one laid down in her bed and drew the quilt up. She went away" (p. 63). Everything is in order if it helps deny Addie's death, and Vardaman denies it desperately right to the end (p. 187).

The metaphor of the fish has been interpreted by most critics with reference to mythology: for some it is a Christian symbol, for others an allusion to the Quest of the Holy Grail, while others go so far as to invoke the dolphin that Greek legend associated with Demeter.[32] In seeking references outside the specific context of the novel, these critics tend to forget the troubled waters in which this fish was hooked. The equation mother=fish must be construed primarily in terms of Vardaman's fantasy, and although the mental process by which it was formed and its immediate practical purpose as a means of magic denial are obvious enough, its significance in Vardaman's emotional experience probably goes beyond that. The fish is in the first instance a metaphor of the mother; it is perhaps not going too far to consider it also as a regressive image of the child. Is a fetus not physiologically a fish in its mother's womb?[33] And would it be so surprising that the loss of his mother reactivated in the boy the desire to be at one with her, the wish to revert to the sheltered life of the embryo? If we retain this hypothesis, it follows that the fish represents both mother and child,[34] and the image should then be read as an expression of prenatal nostalgia, an emblem of the primal union of child and mother Vardaman is unconsciously yearning for. Such an interpretation seems all the more plausible as it fits perfectly into the overall symbolic pattern of the book.

In order to understand the implications of this fantasy in all their ambivalence, it might be useful too to examine more closely the role of the fish in the novel. What strikes us first is Vardaman's aggressiveness toward it: he pokes out one of its eyes, he swears at it (p. 30) as Jewel does at his horse, and instead of gutting it as his father asks, he chops it up with an axe (p. 37). After Addie's death the idea that most preoccupies him is that the fish will be cooked and eaten (p. 55). For Vardaman, eating the fish is an appropriation not only of its flesh but of its vital principle; therefore, as in a totemic meal, it is also a reappropriation of the mother, a transubstantiation of her flesh into the flesh of her kin which guarantees her survival: "And tomorrow it will be cooked and et and she will be him and pa and Cash and Dewey Dell and there wont be anything in the box and so she can breathe" (pp. 63–64). Only the symbolism of the unconscious can help us here, and readers of Melanie Klein will no doubt recognize the links between Vardaman's imaginings and the oral and sadistic fantasies of dismemberment and incorporation brought to light by the psychoanalysis of infantile neuroses.

Stunned though he is, Vardaman is nonetheless among those of the Bundren family who bear the shock best. His sensitivity is as shaken as Darl's, but unlike his brother, he does not succumb to his bewilderment. Like Jewel, Vardaman is active and, as the scene with Peabody's horses shows, capable of physical violence. But what is most striking is the intense mental activity he displays in his monologues. Vardaman sees more than he can understand and formulate; his thoughts, like Dewey Dell's, seem chaotic and become thoroughly unhinged in moments of great emotional stress (cf. sect. 35), yet one feels he is making a stubborn effort to escape from incoherence and conquer his panic. When, in the darkness of the stable, Jewel's horse seems to dissolve, his memory and imagination recreate it straightaway:

> a co-ordinated whole of splotched hide and strong bones within which, detached and secret and familiar, an *is* different from my *is*. . . . I can see hearing coil toward him, caressing, shaping his hard shape—fetlock, hip, shoulder and head; smell and sound. I am not afraid. [p. 55]

Vardaman's monologues trace the tenacious gropings of a child's intelligence towards a firmer hold on reality and towards self-assertion in the face of its disorder. His is a mind still steeped in emotion and imagination, but whose total energies strive feverishly toward order, toward the beginnings of rationality. It is significant that Vardaman constantly feels the need to count (for example, the buzzards), to enumerate, to break any whole down to its constituent parts; thus, instead of "We are walking up the hill," he says "Darl and Jewel and Dewey Dell and I are walking up the hill" (p. 200). Even more revealing is the frequency of grammatical substitutions (repetition of the same sentences with different subjects or predicates, changes of tense, switches to the negative form, etc.) in the course of which he is attempting to assess the differences and similarities:

> Jewel is my brother. Cash is my brother. Cash has a broken leg. We fixed Cash's leg so it doesn't hurt. Cash is my brother. Jewel is my brother too, but he hasn't got a broken leg. [p. 200]

It is obviously no mere chance that the family is the privileged object of these fumbling attempts at analysis. Vardaman is trying to unravel the web of family relationships and determine his own position within the family and with respect to each of its members. In him the apprenticeship of reason goes hand in hand with the search for identity. Is his search as futile as Darl's or Dewey Dell's? Vardaman doubtless ends by discovering his identity, but in the grief of a further loss: "Darl is my brother. Darl. Darl." These are his last words, this his last cry (p. 242). And all the endeavors of this child's intelligence have in no way lessened his perplexity and powerlessness, for they can do nothing against the incurable madness of adults:

> He was a child trying to cope with this adult's world which to him was, and to any sane person, completely mad. . . . He didn't know what to do about it.[35]

6

The Setting

> That's the one trouble with this country: everything, weather, all,
> hangs on too long. Like our rivers, our land: opaque, slow, violent;
> shaping and creating the life of man in its implacable and brooding
> image. [pp. 43–44]

SUCH IS FAULKNER'S EARTH: a space where things are held in
endless abeyance, where nothing has a beginning or an ending; a
viscous, reptilian time, whose treacherous slowness is broken by
sudden outbursts of violence; a nameless and omnipresent force
which has been creating and molding man in its image according
to the same immutable laws for thousands of years. The earth is
the primal matrix, the original crucible in which all life develops,
"the hot blind earth" in which the wet seed germinates (p. 61);
it is also "the dead earth in the dead darkness" (p. 61), the ultimate dust to which all life descends. As Harry Wilbourne says in
The Wild Palms: "Grave-womb or womb-grave, it's all one."[1]

Man is born of mud. A manifold complicity binds him to the
soil which bears and nourishes him, to the powers of sun, night,
fire, water, and wind. Yet this complicity is first and foremost that
of an age-old struggle. The peasant knows this better than anyone, since he confronts the earth in his daily work and has learned
to beware of its wild and cunning whims: "It's a hard country on
man; it's hard" (p. 104). Like all Faulkner's novels, *As I Lay*

Dying pits man against the world around him, against what the novelist used to call his environment. But the conflict is reduced here to its most elementary form. The world against which the Bundrens measure themselves has little in common with the one full of social, racial, and historical fatality in which the destiny of Faulkner's patrician families is played out. Their immediate opponent is Nature, and as in "Old Man" it is against her—against the fury of elements, against the violence of fire and water—that the battle is waged.

The setting for the action is therefore far from being an inert backdrop before which the characters come and act out their drama. It is an agent in its own right and on the same footing as the characters. If we momentarily leave aside its psychological and philosophical complexities and consider *As I Lay Dying* in its epic or allegorical simplicity, little remains but the description of Man—a collective hero represented both by the Bundren family and by the farmers who lend a hand—locked in single combat with Nature. And so close is their embrace that the two adversaries can be hardly distinguished from each other. The traditional distinction between character and setting thus becomes nearly pointless.[2] The scene comes to life and takes part in the action; conversely, the characters tend to lose their individual outlines and to blend with the landscape. This tendency to describe men and things as if they were cut from the same cloth is frequent in Faulkner; perhaps it is even more conspicuous in *As I Lay Dying* than in the other novels. Here all barriers between the animate and the inanimate, the human and the nonhuman, the subjective and the objective, are removed: the world is within man, and man is everywhere within the world.

Stasis and Motion

The strangeness of this magical universe manifests itself first of all in a perpetual oscillation between movement and immobility, in their irresoluble contradiction. *As I Lay Dying* depicts moving figures in a space which is itself moving: the Bundrens' wagon trundles obstinately along the road; Jewel wheels on horseback around the funeral cortège; the buzzards circle in the July sky. But nature also moves: a storm bursts, torrential rain sweeps down, the river overflows and its raging water carries all before it. Few of Faulkner's novels give so intensely the sensation of a seething world, and rarely does the novelist keep his paradoxical wager better: "to arrest motion, which is life, by artificial means and hold it fixed so that a hundred years later, when a stranger looks at it, it moves again, since it is life."[3]

Some passages in the book are pure kinetic poems. Consider for instance this lyrical evocation of Jewel and his horse:

> When Jewel can almost touch him, the horse stands on his hind legs and slashes down at Jewel. Then Jewel is enclosed by a glittering maze of hooves as by an illusion of wings; among them, beneath the upreared chest, he moves with the flashing limberness of a snake. For an instant before the jerk comes onto his arms he sees his whole body earth-free, horizontal, whipping snake-limber, until he finds the horse's nostrils and touches earth again. [p. 12][4]

Yet as much as by movement, Faulkner seems fascinated by immobility (the word "motionless" recurs many times in the novel). Or rather what fascinates him is the passage, sudden or imperceptible, from one to the other, as the continuation of the above extract shows: "Then they are rigid, motionless, terrific" (p. 12). Any movement is followed by a halt. In Faulkner, however, immobility is scarcely ever absolute or final. Stillness is almost always throbbing with latent motion; it is movement beginning or ending, energy dying or gathering its forces. Often it is simply the lull before the storm:

> They stand in terrific hiatus, the horse trembling and groaning. Then Jewel is on the horse's back. He flows upward in a stooping swirl like the lash of a whip, his body in midair shaped to the horse. [p. 12]

This leads us to the self-contradictory concept, well attested in literature and especially in the plastic arts so often referred to by Faulkner, of "dynamic immobility." Darl uses this very expression when describing Cash at work:

> Cash works on, half turned into the feeble light, one thigh and one pole-thin arm braced, his face sloped into the light with a rapt, dynamic immobility above his tireless elbow. [p. 72]

The moment described here is one of those "frozen moments"[5]— frequent in Faulkner's work and of which there are some fine examples in *As I Lay Dying*—when characters turn into statues and the scene suddenly becomes a tableau. They are equivocal moments (like stills inserted into film sequences by some modern directors) suggestive of the continuation of movement even while arresting it; moments of suspension set apart from the flux of time and, as it were, from reality itself (cf. p. 211: "They are like two figures in a Greek frieze, isolated out of all reality by the red glare"). If so many scenes seem to dissolve into unreality, it is because immobility and motion are equally deceptive appearances. Any immobility is false immobility; any movement becomes mere make-believe. Before Vardaman's eyes, Peabody's horses wheel without moving, like horses on a merry-go-round:

> I strike at them, striking, they wheeling in a long lunge, the buggy wheeling onto two wheels and motionless like it is nailed to the ground and the horses motionless like they are nailed by the hind feet to the center of a whirling plate. [p. 54]

The riddle of motion and immobility is the spatial and physical translation of the metaphysical enigma of time and timelessness. This is probably the reason that Faulkner finds it so exciting. Again and again he reverts to it and attempts to capture it in words. And there are moments indeed when revelation seems near. In *As I Lay Dying,* as in the opening pages of *Light in August* depicting Lena Grove's progress on the road to Jefferson, it happens that the paradoxical conjunction of motion and stasis reaches a kind of perfection, that motion becomes so slow as to be the mere tremor of immobility. Then space and time exchange their attributes; time becomes space, space time—not the time of events but a time accumulated like that of memory, bewitched like that of dreams, fluid and static; a time marking time. As Darl, sitting on the wagon, watches Jewel on his horse, the road between them no longer measures distance but time:

> We go on with a motion so soporific, so dreamlike as to be uninferant of progress, as though time and not space were decreasing between us and it. [p. 101]

Similarly, at the time of the crossing, when Darl is looking at his family on the other bank, the separating interval seems temporal rather than spatial:

> It is as though the space between us were time: an irrevocable quality. It is as though time, no longer running straight before us in a diminishing line, now runs parallel between us like a looping string, the distance being the doubling accretion of the thread and not the interval between. [p. 139][6]

METAMORPHOSIS

THROUGH this baffling dialectic of space and time, through this giddy interplay of stasis and motion, in which reality is no sooner mentioned than it is conjured away, Faulkner's universe offers us one of its central paradoxes: dynamic immobility, petrified turbulence, "fury in itself quiet with stagnation" (p. 156).

In *As I Lay Dying* this paradox assumes cosmic proportions; the novel often suggests a world threatened by paralysis, on the point of lapsing back into inertia, nearing its end, yet at the same time, as we have already noted, it also conveys a sensation of prodigious activity. Motion, what Darl calls "the myriad original motion" (p. 156), is at work not only across the universe but in the universe, in the heart of the elements, substances and beings that it compels to transform themselves, sweeping them along in the flux of incessant change. Nothing has yet been fixed in its function and identity; everything is fleeting and flowing. Metamorphosis governs all.

The climactic river scene is the most revealing in this respect. Water, the element of metamorphosis *par excellence,* springs to life. Tull, for instance, describes it in the following way:

> The water was cold. It was thick, like slush ice. Only it kind of lived. One part of you knowed it was just water, the same thing that had been running under this same bridge for a long time, yet when them logs would come spewing up outen it, you were not surprised, like they was a part of water, of the waiting and the threat. [p. 131]

The same animism even more markedly informs Darl's description of the scene. Beneath the murmuring, swirling surface of the water, Darl senses the disturbing presence of some marine monster up from the deep, a slumbering Leviathan which moves in its sleep and threatens to wake at any moment:

> Before us the thick dark current runs. It talks up to us in a murmur become ceaseless and myriad, the yellow surface dimpled monstrously into fading swirls travelling along the surface for an instant, silent, impermanent and profoundly significant, as though just beneath the surface something huge and alive waked for a moment of lazy alertness out of and into light slumber again. [p. 134]

Immediately after, the foam turns to sweat, the river becomes a galloping horse:

> It clucks and murmurs among the spokes and about the mules' knees, yellow, skummed with flotsam and with thick soiled gouts of foam as though it had sweat, lathering, like a driven horse. [p. 134]

And once in the water, Darl feels as if his body is being kneaded by invisible hands: "It is like hands molding and prodding at the very bones" (p. 151).

Nothing, it seems, is left to define the hierarchy of nature's categories, or to distinguish reality from unreality. The inanimate comes to life, matter becomes dematerialized and ghostlike: a log surges out of the water, standing "for an instant upright upon that surging and heaving desolation like Christ" (p. 141), and "upon the end of it a long gout of foam hangs like the beard of an old man or a goat" (p. 141). Men turn into animals, looking like birds, dogs, horses, or cattle,[7] while animals become human. The buzzard Samson sees in his barn after the Bundrens have left is almost taken to be a human being, and he watches it go away like "a old bald-headed man" (p. 112). Jewel's horse, during the river crossing, flounders in the water, "moaning and groaning like a natural man" (p. 147). It is particularly in the teeth of disaster and death that the kinship of man and beast is acknowledged; they communicate then in their common terror and, in *As I Lay Dying* as in Picasso's *Guernica,* are seen to adopt identical attitudes and expressions. All the world's anguish is reflected in the mules' sad and terrified eyes:

> Looking back once, their gaze sweeps across us with in their eyes a wild, sad, profound and despairing quality as though they had already seen in the thick water the shape of the disaster which they could not speak and we could not see. [p. 139]

And this is how Darl evokes the last look and cry of a drowning mule:

> The head of one mule appears, its eyes wide; it looks back at us for an instant, making a sound almost human. The head vanishes again. [p. 142]

Between man and animal, as between man and things, continual and unpredictable exchanges of properties occur. *As I Lay Dying* sucks us into the whirlpool of a protean world whose only law seems to be change and which achieves unity only through the countless analogies these exchanges tirelessly weave between one realm and another. From metaphor one moves to metamorphosis and from metamorphosis back to metaphor: everything becomes "profoundly significant" (p. 134); not only *are* things something other than themselves, but they *say* something else as well. Everything cross-refers to everything else through a mysterious network of often startlingly close correspondences. Thus the dead fish hiding in the dust, "like it was ashamed of being dead, like it was in a hurry to get back hid again" (p. 30), foreshadows "that pride, that furious desire to hide that abject nakedness which we bring here with us" (p. 44) of which Peabody speaks with regard to Addie. And the sun, "a bloody egg upon a crest of thunderheads," the evening of the storm, is like a cosmic counterpart to Addie's corpse, a broken egg in her coffin (p. 39).

The most disturbing feature is not that inert objects enjoy a strange life of their own, but that this strangeness has something human about it in which man recognizes obscurely the image of his own destiny. Even the random shapes of nature sometimes resemble human ones, as in this sentence where the configuration of the place suddenly appears like the sketch of some anatomy: "The path looks like a crooked limb blown against the bluff" (p. 41). The human figure in return sometimes seems to reproduce the shapes and forces of the universe. Dewey Dell, as we have seen, is described by Darl as a miniature cosmos; her "mammalian ludicrosities" are "the horizons and the valleys of the earth," (p. 156) and her leg "measures the length and breadth of life" (p. 98). The human and the cosmic are in the relationship of reciprocal metaphor. In this fluctuating world everything thus ends by being absorbed into the unity of a single vision.

THE APOCALYPSE

ALL this turmoil might presage the birth of a new cosmos. Yet it does not take us long to discover that there is no question here of a genesis. The world depicted in *As I Lay Dying* is not one emerging from primeval chaos but one preparing to return to it.

In the first sections, it is true, we are still on firm ground, in a clearly ordered space which the eye can master and take in and size up at its leisure. Darl's opening monologue describes the setting with an almost geometrical precision (pp. 3–4). But soon the scene starts to crack up, and we slip into an unfamiliar dimension, where the ordinary laws of perception no longer obtain. The acoustics are upset: in the Bundrens' house on the hill sounds travel most oddly; voices are heard nearby, disembodied and sourceless: "As you enter the hall, they sound as though they were speaking out of the air about you" (p. 19). Sounds have a strange habit especially of "ceasing without departing":

> Cash labors about the trestles, moving back and forth, lifting and placing the planks with long clattering reverberations in the dead air as though he were lifting and dropping them at the bottom of an invisible well, the sounds ceasing without departing, as if any movement might dislodge them from the immediate air in reverberant repetition. [pp. 71–72]

By some inexplicable power of remanence, sounds linger in endless reverberation, remain as traces even when they are no longer audible. Everything that strikes the senses seems destined to persist beyond its disappearance. Few words in this novel recur more often than "fading": nothing is ever fully present, nothing completely vanishes; sounds and sights are in a state of perpetual suspension, oscillating between receding presence and nearby absence, as can be also seen from Darl's singular description of shadows:

> Upon the impalpable plane of [the air] their shadows form as upon a wall, as though like sound they had not gone very far away in falling but had merely congealed for a moment immediate and musing. [p. 72]

Concrete things are dematerialized; shadows acquire substance. A similar phenomenon occurs in the scene where the Bundren brothers carry Addie's coffin to the wagon; when the "box" slips from Darl's hands, it slides "down the air like a sled upon invisible snow, smoothly evacuating atmosphere in which the sense of it is still shaped" (p. 92). And just as sounds, shadows, and objects do, so events leave a wake: after the crossing, when the wagon has finally been hauled out of the river, "it is as though upon the shabby, familiar, inert shape of the wagon there lingered somehow, latent yet immediate, that violence which had slain the mules that drew it not an hour since" (p. 150).

Another significant anomaly, particularly evident in the night scenes, is the frequent reduction of space to two dimensions. For transparent space in which perspectives are clearly ordered is substituted an opaque space, with neither depth nor relief, against which objects appear flat. In the scene of Addie's death this flattening is twice suggested: when Vardaman leaves the bedside, we see his pale face "fading into the dusk like a piece of paper pasted on a failing wall" (p. 48),[8] and a page later, the dying woman's face is similarly blurred in the twilight, floating in the darkness, "detached upon it, lightly as the reflection of a dead leaf" (p. 49). This transformation of volumes into surfaces is particularly noticeable with regard to characters, who are sometimes reduced by Faulkner to the insubstantial fragility of silhouettes.[9] But it is also to be found in descriptions of the setting. Thus, in the other night scene, which shows us Cash busy finishing the coffin, one finds the following simile: "Upon the dark ground the chips look like random smears of soft pale paint on a black canvas" (p. 71). As in the death scene, space is reduced to two dimensions, but the chromatic range is likewise reduced to two contrasted shades: pale strokes on a black background. The allusion to painting is again revealing; it refers us back to a world of fiction and illusion, one which vacillates between reality and the representation of reality.

This breakdown of perceptions, these distortions of space may be found in many of Faulkner's books, yet rarely have they been used to better effect. Added to so many other suggestions of impending chaos, these singularities are most useful in heightening the apocalyptic atmosphere peculiar to *As I Lay Dying*. This atmosphere already pervades the scene in the opening sections; as in Shakespeare's tragedies, the world seems to be out of joint and is presented from the beginning in an eerie light. Nature holds its breath in expectation of the catastrophe portended by the sinister omens everywhere visible. Before Addie's death, the storm gathers, threatening, on the horizon; light takes on a copper hue, the air smells of sulphur, and the sun is covered with blood (p. 39). The hallucinating night scene already quoted, where Cash saws the last planks for the coffin by the feeble light of a lantern (pp. 71–75), is similarly Shakespearean: the atmosphere is electric; noises, lights, shadows, and the whole landscape assume a supernatural aspect, and again there is the reek of sulphur. Hell is not far away.

As I Lay Dying conjures up Hell as much as the Last Judgment. *Another* world, beyond the range of normal experience, fabulous and terrifying, comes to life, and one cannot tell whether it is given up to demoniacal violence, to the wrath of the Old Testament God, or to the cruel whims of that evil demiurge whom Faulkner sometimes invokes in his novels. When the rain, awaited and feared for so long, finally starts to fall, it sweeps down with a sudden violence suggestive of the biblical Deluge: the drops are "big as buckshot, warm as though fired from a gun; they sweep across the lantern in a vicious hissing" (p. 72). The rainstorm is the first manifestation of the cosmic forces which are going to be unleashed against the Bundrens. It might also be a warning against the folly of their undertaking, like the signpost at a turning of the road which "wheels up like a motionless hand lifted above the profound desolation of the ocean" (p. 102). These dark omens announce the coming catastrophe and proclaim the imminence of the descent into Hell. The wagon is soon to become Charon's ferry: the river crossing, like that of the Styx or Acheron, marks the Bundrens' entry into the underworld. We are now in Death's other kingdom. Everything points to its menacing presence: Addie's coffin swallowed by the raging floodwaters, the floating corpses of pigs and mules (pp. 142, 148), the desolate, haunted wasteland around them ("desolation" and "spectral" recur several times in section 34). The accounts given by the principal witnesses of the scene complement and confirm each other; Darl, the visionary dreamer, and Tull, the man of earthy common sense, both give the impression of escaping from an unprecedented cataclysm. Darl describes the scene as an Apocalypse:

> that single monotony of desolation leaning with that terrific quality a little from right to left, as though we had reached the place where the motion of the wasted world accelerates just before the final precipice. [p. 139]

Tull speaks as someone who has seen the jaws of Hell open:

> The bridge shaking and swaying under us, going down into the moiling water like it went clean through to the other side of the earth, and the other end coming outen the water like it wasn't the same bridge a-tall and that them that would walk up outen the water on that side must come from the bottom of the earth. [pp. 130–131]

The fiendish savagery of the elements reaches a paroxysm here. For the Bundrens it is the decisive ordeal. Not the last, of course, since after the ordeal by water they have to undergo the ordeal by fire. But Darl's description of the barn fire does not have the same sustained apocalyptic intensity; it is more spectacular than visionary, and attention focuses more on the heroic figure of Jewel than on the scene itself, as though man had momentarily regained the upper hand over the elements.

Water rather than fire seems to be the dominant element in *As I Lay Dying*. For it is water that translates most appropriately into the register of the perceptible the obsession with chaos and death which wells up from the whole novel. Water is not simply the prime agent for metamorphosis; while allowing changes of form, it also contains the threat of a regression to the formless. As in "Old Man," the Apocalypse is envisioned here as a liquid catastrophe, and as in *The Sound and the Fury* and *Sanctuary* images of dissolution recur so often that they become one of the significant motifs of the novel. The motif appears first in section 12, in connection with Addie's death:

a runnel of yellow neither water nor earth swirls, curving with the yellow road neither of earth nor water, down the hill dissolving into a streaming mass of dark green neither of earth nor sky. [p. 48]

The confusion of elements is also noted by Tull:

a fellow couldn't tell where was the river and where the land. It was just a tangle of yellow. . . . [p. 118]

Vardaman takes up the motif in his description of the horse:

It is as though the dark were resolving him out of his integrity, into an unrelated scattering of components. . . . I see him dissolve . . . and float upon the dark in fading solution. [p. 55]

The danger of dissolution is also a permanent threat to man, as can be seen in Darl's description of Cash, after the latter has been rescued from the flooded river. Although Cash has not been in the river for more than a few moments, it looks as if the insidious erosion of water had already started corrupting his flesh:

His face appears sunken a little, sagging from the bony ridges of eye sockets, nose, gums, as though the wetting had slacked the firmness which had held the skin full. [p. 149]

For Darl the human body is nothing but an ephemeral "clotting," likely to dissolve at a moment's notice into "the myriad original motion" (p. 156).

Dissolving may be connected with another motif in the novel: uprooting. Each existence draws its life-force from the earth, and the most eloquent symbol of life in *As I Lay Dying* is the "wet seed wild in the hot blind earth" (p. 61). Dying, then, means being torn from the native soil, and Addie's death certainly suggests such an uprooting: Jewel compares his mother's hands to unearthed roots (p. 15), and when she dies, her face seems to float in the dusk, light and detached, like "the reflection of a dead leaf" (p. 49). Significantly enough, it is in Darl's monologues that references to uprooting or, more generally, to a loss of contact with the earth are most numerous. Almost all of them occur in sections 34 and 37, where he relates the river episode and its consequences:

> Above the ceaseless surface they stand—trees, cane, vines—*rootless, severed from the earth*. . . . [p. 135]
> as if the road too had been *soaked free of earth* and floated upward. . . . [p. 136]
> [the drowned mules'] legs stiffly extended as when *they had lost contact with the earth*. [p. 142]
> Jewel and Vernon are in the river again. From here they do not appear to violate the surface at all; it is as though it had *severed* them both at a single blow. . . . [p. 156]

That Darl should see images of uprooting everywhere need not surprise us: they reflect his own rootlessness. Similarly, the world of metamorphosis mirrors his nonidentity and the vision of the Apocalypse his inner collapse. Through the scenes he describes it is his own vertigo he tries to pinpoint and fix in words. In *As I Lay Dying* no space is uninhabited, for every place here is haunted by the presence of a consciousness. The characters project themselves into the landscape and make it throb with their desires and anxieties. Thus Dewey Dell finds signs of her expectancy in everything she sees, whether a pine clump (p. 59) or a signboard (p. 114). It is true that reality is not interiorized to the same extent in all the monologues; the theater in which the drama is enacted is not a mere shadow theater, and the scene eventually acquires, thanks mostly to the contribution of the peripheral narrators, a semblance of objective existence. Yet it is through the descriptions most charged with subjectivity that the setting is made memorable. Darl's combine the quiver of sensitivity with an unfailing acuity of perception. In the novel he stages the show. Through his eyes the scenery leaps to life. It is not enough to say that his evocations are the richest and most suggestive. The setting of the book is invented in his look, created through his words.

7

Themes

DEATH AND MADNESS

THE THEMATICS of *As I Lay Dying* are tantalizingly elusive, yet a valuable clue is provided from the outset by the very title of the novel. Ambiguous, like many of Faulkner's titles,[1] it does not apply to the book in its entirety if taken literally, for only the first third of the narrative is devoted to Addie Bundren's agony; the implication is that the heroine actually never stops dying throughout the journey, and only meets death when she is eventually buried at Jefferson. In other words, the whole novel deals with an almost endless agony, a prolonged suspension between life and death. What it is concerned with is not so much death as the process of dying, not so much death as a brute fact as its mute presence in the very heart of life. *As I Lay Dying* works from the start with the double paradox of a dying life and an active death.

Life and death are not opposed here as being and nothingness, but combine in a relationship of exchange and mutual inclusion, communicating in the undivided zone of their common frontier. This central ambiguity is echoed by the motif, perceptible at various levels, of the *in-between*. First, the in-between nature of the work itself, which, as has been seen, hesitates between several genres and various tonalities without ever settling for one.[2] The scene of the action similarly unfolds between two worlds, in a space both moving and immobile, animated and inert, infernal and earthly, and whose beginning and end are confused;[3] a space between day and night, at the uncertain hour of twilight:[4] as in *The Sound and the Fury*—whose original title was *Twilight*—the novelist associates death with the dying of the day by making Addie's last moments coincide with nightfall (cf. pp. 47, 49). In the chiaroscuro of this ambiguous world, things and beings are in a state of constant flux; there is nothing one can be sure of, and even death itself becomes uncertain. Addie has not yet passed on when she is referred to in the past tense, as if she were already dead; and after she has been nailed in her coffin for several days her family treats her as if she were still alive. And we even hear her voice when buzzards have started wheeling above her rotting corpse.

It is precisely the *corpse* which offers us the most arresting image of the impossible separation of life and death. In the corpse, death becomes visible and reveals itself as the degradation of the human body into an inert object. A fascinating object, certainly, insofar as "the corpse is its own image,"[5] linked with living flesh in a relationship of perfect resemblance and absolute difference; a disquieting and distressing object which materializes the unreal and gives absence a face; an incongruous object, too, as if come from elsewhere, and one which is *de trop* in our world. Therefore nothing appears more urgent to the living than to make the corpse disappear. In *As I Lay Dying,* however, everything happens as though it either could not or would not disappear. The time separating the corpse's first appearance and its burial is prolonged to excess, beyond tolerable bounds (Faulkner makes use of a similar situation in "A Rose for Emily"), and the ordinary course of events is thus profoundly disturbed. The Bundrens' problem is not unlike Amédée's in Ionesco's play of the same name: how to get rid of it? Only at the end of a long and perilous journey will they succeed in disposing of their mother's body. Meanwhile, they are forced to live daily next to a cumbrous and stubborn corpse.

All the book's action revolves around the unburied remains of Addie Bundren. *As I Lay Dying* is first and foremost the story of a family struggling with a corpse, the story of an unburiable cadaver,[6] and most of the ordeals encountered on the journey stem directly from the material difficulties of carting the body to the graveyard at Jefferson. Death therefore comes to impinge on the banal practical problems of everyday life. For the Bundrens, the corpse is not so much an object of horror and revulsion as a nuisance. By their continual manipulation of the coffin, they almost reach the point where it is considered a mere load to be carried. They are too absorbed by their immediate task to realize how shocking the unduly prolonged presence of a rotting corpse may be to others; they even forget its nauseating smell, which attracts buzzards and repels people. To this guileless scorn of decorum and convention, this obstinate failure of realization, this seemingly unruffled innocence in the face of death the story owes much of its baffling extravagance. Apart from Darl and perhaps Cash, none of the Bundrens appear to be conscious of the outrageous nature of the journey. Behind their blindness, however, we discover another form of blindness: the feigned blindness of the author, pretending not to see the scandal. For, all the way, Faulkner's humor keeps death at a distance. As in the grotesque wake scene in *Sanctuary,* he desacralizes the corpse by treating it as a mere object and defuses the Gothic potential by farce.

Yet, as the doctor-*cum*-philosopher Peabody says, death is a "function of the mind" before being a "phenomenon of the body" (p. 42). The attitude of the Bundrens toward Addie's corpse is not simply a pretext for macabre humor; it claims our attention most of all because of what it reveals about their attitude toward death itself. And this again is utterly ambiguous: in the familiarity between living and dead, it would be wrong to see nothing but the effect of habit; what it points to is a kind of weird intimacy which precludes neither respect, fear, nor piety, and through which emerge recognizable traces of that ancient belief which has it that the dead continue to live—for a certain time at least—parallel lives to our own.[7] The Bundrens, as has already been noted, speak of Addie as if she were still alive, attributing needs, thoughts, and intentions to her; it is her presence, felt by everyone, that keeps the family together during the journey, and it is to all appearances her imperious will that makes them carry the task through to the end. In answer to Tull, who shows surprise at his haste and obstinacy, Anse says (no doubt hypocritically): "I gave my promise. . . . She is counting on it" (p. 133). In almost every member of the family may be detected, if not the certainty, at least the suspicion of an afterlife for Addie, and little Vardaman even goes so far as to make holes in the coffin to allow his mother to breathe.

For these primitives, then, there is no dividing line between life and death. In the magic universe which is theirs, "every death is analogous to a change of birth, every birth analogous to a change of death, every change analogous to a death-rebirth—and the cycle of human life is analogous to the natural cycles of death and rebirth."[8] The whole of Faulkner's work revolves in the ever renewed cycle of gestations and agonies, but in few of his novels are death and birth as closely interwoven as in *As I Lay Dying*. And none perhaps is as firmly rooted in the primal earth of the archaic mind, for it is, as we shall see, to archetypal image-patterns that the death-birth theme owes its most eloquent symbols.

That at the center of this thematic development we should find again the enigmatic figure of Addie Bundren is hardly surprising. Addie is the dead person among the living, as well as being the mother among her children. This association of motherhood and death[9] could not be more strongly emphasized than it is in her monologue: her whole existence has been dominated by the obsession with death and haunted by sex and childbirth. These obsessions recur, a generation later, to differing degrees of intensity and in different modes of perception, in her children, and particularly in the ones she loved least: Dewey Dell, Vardaman, and Darl. Vardaman's panic at discovering the mystery of death is paralleled by Dewey Dell's scandalized stupor at the mystery of burgeoning life. As for Darl, Addie's death plunges him into the same anguish; it repeats in a way the trauma of his birth, materializes the frustration he has never stopped feeling ever since, and it is almost as if he were losing his mother for a second time. It is in him, because he is to some extent the reembodiment of Addie's restless consciousness, that her twin obsessions come together again to merge into the obsession with time and the end of time. His whole vision is marked by it. The world in his view is sometimes a world in gestation, and every tree then becomes a tree of life:

the trees, motionless, are ruffled out to the last twig, swollen, increased, as though quick with young [p. 72],[10]

sometimes a world in agony, teetering on the brink of the abyss:

that single monotony of desolation leaning with that terrified quality a little from right to left, as though we had reached the place where the motion of the wasted world accelerates just before the final precipice. [p. 139]

Suspended between the moment of generation and the moment of death, a mere flicker between two eternities of darkness, all existence seems to Darl like a meaningless countdown; in each man's destiny he sees the prefiguration of the final cataclysm:

It takes two people to make you, and one people to die. That's how the world is going to end. [p. 38]

Elsewhere, the obsession is fixed in imagery:

The sun, an hour above the horizon, is poised like a bloody egg upon a crest of thunderheads; the light has turned copper: in the

eye portentous, in the nose sulphurous, smelling of lightning.
[p. 39]

The association here of the sun and the organic images of blood and the egg condenses the birth-death theme in a single symbolic fulguration.[11] It could be the start of a cosmogonic reverie: sun, blood, egg, are these not first of all emblems of fecundity and promises of life? In this sulphurous and sinister atmosphere, however, the meaning is reversed: the sun is declining, the bloody egg is broken, the landscape changes into an apocalyptic vision.

This ambiguous symbolism does not only pervade the imagery of the novel, it also underlies its narrative pattern. *As I Lay Dying* is the tale of a *journey*—a symbol of life and death for the primitive mind as well as for the child[12] or the dreamer. From this archetypal metaphor derives, parallel to the real action, the symbolic and ritual action which gives the novel its mythical dimension. "The structural metaphor in *As I Lay Dying* is," as Hyatt H. Waggoner puts it, "a journey through life to death and through death to life."[13]

First there is Addie's last journey bearing her body back to the land of her birth and ancestors. This return takes place under the sign of birth, sex, death, and that which encompasses them all: time. The coffin is shaped like a grandfather clock; Addie is placed in it head to foot, like a child in its mother's womb at birth, and she is wearing her bridal dress (cf. pp. 82–83).[14] The "box" Cash made for her is thus simultaneously coffin, womb, and marriage bed. As for Addie's funeral journey itself, it is almost like a repetition of her restless life. As Rabi has pointed out, her posthumous adventures recall "the distant tribulations of folklore, where we see the dead painfully reaching the kingdom of souls after a journey full of terrible events."[15] Everything happens as if the elements were disputing Addie's corpse: air (the possibility of the body being left prey to the buzzards), water (the coffin immersed in the river), fire (cremation narrowly avoided in the fire scene), and earth, in which the dead woman is eventually buried, none of the "four countries of death"[16] is missing from the novel. For Addie, the passage from life to death is not just the matter of a moment but a long quest strewn with ambushes and perils, like the funeral crossings of myth and legend.

The convoy making for Jefferson thus brings to mind the ferries of the Egyptians and the Greeks as well as the phantom chariots of Celtic and Scandinavian folklore. The journey is the passage from one world to another, and in *As I Lay Dying* this applies not only to the dead but also to the living. The funeral rite is mirrored by an initiation rite which brings the Bundren children face to face with the twin enigmas of life and death. One needs only to glance through an anthropological study like Mircea Eliade's *Birth and Rebirth*[17] to realize how close the correspondences between the novel and such ritual patterns are. As in many initiation rites, the action begins with a leave-taking from the mother, the brutal expulsion from the sheltered world of childhood. Similarly, the crucial episodes of the journey may be interpreted as reenactments of the ritual ordeals which primitive societies impose on their neophytes. The decisive trial is by water, whose symbolic multivalence is so hauntingly brought to life in Darl's description of the river scene. The water rushes along with destructive violence, drowning pigs and mules and threatening to engulf all the Bundrens. But however masculine its fury, the river is also a symbol of cosmic motherhood. Mixed with the earth—the water is muddy, black or yellow—and therefore doubly feminine, it represents the primordial matter (*materia* = that which belongs to the mother) in which all life is made and unmade. And the fact that Addie's coffin is swallowed up and almost carried away by the current (Vardaman says his mother moves like a fish in the water) confirms, if confirmation is needed, its maternal character.[18] If the rite begins with a break from the mother, it is paradoxically a return to the mother-womb as well. The immersion of the three elder sons during the crossing of the river marks the regression to a prenatal limbo; like

"Jewel," I say. Overhead the day drives level and gray, hiding the sun by a flight of gray spears. In the rain the mules smoke a little, splashed yellow with mud, the off one clinging in sliding lunges to the side of the road. The tilted lumber gleams dull yellow, water-soaked and heavy as lead, tilted at a steep angle into the ditch, above the broken wheel, about the shattered spokes [and about Jewel's ~ankles~ straining ankles] a runnel of ~yellow water swirls~ yellow neither of water nor earth, swirls, curving with the yellow road neither of water nor earth, down the hill [dissolving into ~a dark mass of~ a streaming mass of dark green neither of earth nor sky]. ~Jewel's hat droops about his neck, channeling water onto the towsack wrapped about his shoulders as, ankle-deep in the running ditch, he pries with a slipping 2 × 4 at the axel~ "Jewel," I say.

Cash came to the door, carrying the ~adze~ saw. (?) Pa stood beside the bed, humped, his arms dangling.

all baptismal ceremonies, it is at once a symbolic death and a rebirth.[19] To conquer their new identities, the neophytes must cross the river of Hell and, under the guidance of the Great Earth Mother, enter that shadowy other world which is both the dwelling of souls to be born and the kingdom of the dead.

All these ritual connotations, however, should not be confused with the meaning of the novel as such. Whether a funeral rite or an initiation rite is at play, irony joins in, surreptitiously paring away its traditional significance. Hence some further ambiguities: insofar as the novel lays itself open to the timeless dimension of myth, it implicitly refers to those "old universal truths lacking which any story is ephemeral and doomed,"[20] but as the symbolic expression of a world order and a relationship to truth, the rite is immediately devalued. Addie's tribulations are, after all, only those of a decaying corpse, and the funeral rite itself, when one thinks of all the secret selfish reasons the Bundrens have for going to Jefferson, tends to become a grotesque travesty.[21] As much can be said of the initiation rite: for none of the Bundren children does it lead to a genuine rebirth. At the end of the journey Dewey Dell and Vardaman are as bemused as ever; Cash, despite his stoical acceptance of suffering, is still his former self; to Jewel the ordeals have given an opportunity to test his heroic valiance, but he has gone through them with wooden rigidity, impervious and unchanged. As for Darl, he emerges from the river with empty hands (p. 144). The experience of the journey has altered him indeed, but hardly for the better: his anguished search for an identity has led to nothing but despair and madness.

As with death, madness is always just around the corner throughout the novel. If *The Sound and the Fury* is "a tale told by an idiot, full of sound and fury," *As I Lay Dying* is a tale of madness told by a madman. Madness is everywhere present. It is in the apocalyptic disorder of the world and the unbridled violence of the elements. It is also in the unreason of man: could there be a more senseless undertaking than the Bundrens'? As in

King Lear, human madness thus parallels the madness of the world. Echoing and questioning one another, the multiple forms of madness draw us into another vortex of ambiguities and ironies. The Bundrens' expedition is a fool's errand in the eyes of the community; in the eyes of Vardaman, the child, it is the folly of adults.[22] Yet it is also, paradoxically, madness in the eyes of Darl—who is himself thought to be mad. There must be reason, then, in his madness, a reason that challenges the reason of reasonable people. Hence the difficulty, fully recognized by Cash, of discriminating between reason and unreason:

> Sometimes I ain't so sho who's got ere a right to say when a man is crazy and when he aint. Sometimes I think it aint none of us pure crazy and aint none of us pure sane until the balance of us talks him that-a-way. It's like it aint so much what a fellow does, but it's the way the majority of folks is looking at him when he does it. [p. 223]

Madness only exists by common consent. Any boundary between sanity and insanity is arbitrary. In *As I Lay Dying* the two, like life and death, are so inextricably intertwined that distinction between them proves impossible. Therefore nothing is more ambiguous in the novel than Darl's laughter. During the journey, of all the Bundren family, Darl is the only one to laugh, as he is the only one to cry (cf. p. 215). He laughs for the first time at the outset of the journey (pp. 99–100), the second time when the two state officials come to take him to the insane asylum (pp. 227–28), and lastly when, looking out of the train, he sees his family by the wagon, about to leave for home (pp. 243–44). What is the motive for Darl's laughter? He himself does not seem to know: "What are you laughing at?" he wonders. Is it at himself (of whom he speaks at the end of the novel in the third person, as if he were *someone else*), at his ludicrous family, or at both together? Is this the hysterical laughter of madness or that of reason confronted with the absurd spectacle of an insane world?[23] In the closing pages of *The Sound and the Fury* Benjy bellows because things are out of order; Darl laughs because things fall back into order: the Bundrens have accomplished their mission, Addie is buried and about to be replaced by the "duck-shaped" woman, and Darl will soon be in his rightful place among the madmen, inside the asylum walls. "Down there it'll be quiet," Cash tells him reassuringly, "with none of the bothering and such. It'll be better for you" (p. 228). But is this restoration of order not more derisory and revolting than disorder?

Darl questions himself three times on what it is that makes him laugh, and in the "you" of his queries the reader has the impression that it is he who is being asked. Darl replies by three series of yeses, which in their turn pose a question, since this repeated "yes," as suspect as Quentin's vehement denial at the end of *Absalom, Absalom!,* only increases our puzzlement. Perhaps Darl expresses a final attempt to cling to life, perhaps his consent to the living death which awaits him at Jackson. Yet one is also tempted to read into these strident affirmations the cruelly ironic expression of refusal, of that "no" that so many of Faulkner's heroes utter in the face of their destiny precisely when they are succumbing to it.

From the depths of his own madness, Darl discovers—and makes us discover—the madness of the universe. It is a discovery which goes hand in hand with that of death: madness and death in *As I Lay Dying* represent the two poles of a single anxiety. Madness appears here, to use Michel Foucault's phrase, as "le déjà-là de la mort" ("the already-here of death").[24] Faulkner has been likened to the medieval painters and sculptors of *danses macabres;*[25] his vision and art have been compared to Brueghel's and Bosch's. *As I Lay Dying* indeed makes one think of the end of the Middle Ages, of that moment of western sensibility when the Ship of Fools came to occupy the place in the imagination previously held by the Dance of Death. This shift from the theme of death to the theme of madnes was not, as Foucault points out, a clean break: "What is in question is still the nothingness of existence, but this nothingness is no longer considered an external, final term, both threat and conclusion; it is experienced from within as the continuous and constant form of existence."[26] In *As I Lay Dying* the two themes are as intimately linked; they crystallize around the two most significant figures in the novel: Addie and Darl. Addie embodies the obsession of death: "I could just remember how my father used to say that the reason for living was to get ready to stay dead a long time" (p. 161). And throughout the book the concrete presence of her rotting corpse acts as a reminder of nothingness as "an external, final term," as "threat and conclusion." In Darl's madness, on the other hand, nothingness is experienced "from within as the continuous and constant form of existence":

> How do our lives ravel out into the no-wind, no-sound, the weary gestures weary recapitulant: echoes of old compulsions with no-hand on no-strings: in sunset we fall into furious attitudes, dead gestures of dolls. [pp. 196–97]

"LIVING IS TERRIBLE": THE SCANDAL

In *As I Lay Dying* it is also in terms of death and madness that one should pose the problem of *identity*. Among the characters of the novel there are those who have seemingly found their identity—Anse, Cash, Jewel—and those who are still seeking it—Darl, Vardaman, and, to a lesser degree, Dewey Dell. The first, however different one from another, are alike in their rigidity and fixity. They are people who give nothing away and allow nobody any purchase on them; they are sparing of their words, like Jewel and Cash, or, like Anse, are content with empty words, which is only another way of saying nothing; they either act or do not act, but in Anse's inertia, just as in Jewel's headlong violence or Cash's passion for work, one senses the same stubborn inflexibility, the same imperviousness. Jewel retains throughout the novel the same petrified air (to be faithful to Faulkner's images one should say "lignified"), and a similar stiffness is discernible in Cash as well: during the storm, he keeps working on the coffin, totally unaffected by the drenching rain, as single-minded and composed as before, the motion of his saw continuing with the regularity of a piston, "as though it and the arm functioned in tranquil conviction that rain was an illusion of the mind" (p. 73). As for Anse, he does nothing, and it is his formidable inertia which acts as his shell. But inside this shell there is only emptiness, just as behind Jewel's wooden mask there is perhaps nothing but wild and blind energy. Only Cash—despite his robot gestures and his seemingly narrow mind—ends by convincing us that he also has a soul. Apart from this one exception, identity seems to be won and preserved only at the cost of a benumbed and deadened consciousness.

Settling on an identity means settling in it. Darl, Vardaman, and Dewey Dell have in common that for them this settling-in process has not yet occurred or cannot occur. Their ego has neither form nor substance and finds it therefore difficult to defend itself against the world's encroachment and aggression. It is in them that what doctor Peabody calls "that abject nakedness which we bring here with us" (p. 44) appears most clearly. The most exposed, the most tragically naked is of course Darl; nobody shelters him, nothing protects him, and he does not even have the pride which drives the others to hide their nakedness. His nakedness is different from but at the same time symmetrical with Dewey Dell's. They are both equally incapable of defining themselves within a proper individuality; they are even deprived of solitude, since their consciousness is constantly drawn outside their being: in Dewey Dell's case, it is caught in the body's opacity; in Darl's, it is dissipated in the void. Yet for each of them it is, fundamentally, the same dispossession of self.

Consciousness without identity or identity without consciousness is ultimately the alternative each of Faulkner's characters is

confronted with. The only choice seems to be between the deadness of identity and the madness of nonidentity. Addie's fate is in
its irony an apt illustration of this: throughout her life she has
passionately sought her true self; she only finds it in death, as a
corpse. Similarly Darl's search finds its paradoxical conclusion in
insanity, since it is only when he is acted upon like an object that
he becomes real to himself—as a madman. Whoever tries to reconcile consciousness and identity discovers in himself the nothingness of existence and finishes either by giving up—as Addie
did in bitter resignation—or by giving way to his vertigo like
Darl. To be without identity is to experience death in life. With
nothing to focus on and to relate to, consciousness is left dangling
in a vacuum; at once caught up in solipsistic self-absorption and
self-torment and threatened by dissolution in the impersonal flux
of time and life, it achieves neither true separateness nor true re-
latedness and is bound to succumb to despair or madness.

From these dangers Anse has safely escaped. He has been
quick to find his identity; the very weight of his inertia provides
him with the aplomb that was denied to Addie and Darl. For his
wife, however, Anse is dead before his death: "And then he died.
He did not even know he was dead" (p. 166). Just as Jewel does
not know that he *is,* Anse will never realize that he is "dead."
Both of them are deficient in consciousness and seem to owe their
being to the very fact of their unawareness; as Darl would say,
they are because they don't know they are. Their *sum* implies no
cogito; it does not refer to the transcendence of an ego infused
with the certainty of its own existence; it is somehow exterior to
them, an objective identity like that of things, compact and closed.

Not to be conscious of oneself may also be equated with non-
entity, and identity established at this cost is also a form of death-
in-life—death not by disintegration this time but by congealing.
And it is a form of madness too. In *As I Lay Dying* madness is
prowling everywhere and Darl is not its only prey. There is the
madness of distracted subjectivity, but the lack of inwardness is

also a kind of insanity. The novel exemplifies both categories. The first is pathetic with Vardaman and Dewey Dell, tragic with Darl and Addie; the second, although shown in a comic light, is no less disturbing. Kierkegaard, one of the first to speak of this "objective" madness, noted in this respect:

> This type of madness is more inhuman than the other. One shrinks from looking into the eyes of a madman of the former type lest one be compelled to plumb there the depths of his delirium; but one dares not look at a madman of the latter type at all, from fear of discovering that he has eyes of glass and hair made from carpet-rags. . . .[27]

It is only a short step from these glass eyes to Anse's cinder eyes. Yet in Faulkner's novels objectification is scarcely ever equivalent to a total dehumanization and its significance is not necessarily negative. Anse's appalling callousness, for instance, should not be confused with Cash's imperviousness, although the two characters are alike in their outward grotesqueness. Moreover, it is noteworthy that the least conscious are generally among those who endure and survive. Objectification might then be interpreted rather as a way of taking up fate's challenge and making one immune to its blows, a paradoxical ruse on the part of man's freedom to forestall any danger which, from within or without, threatens to submerge and destroy it. Playing possum becomes a strategy of survival, feigning death a victory over death. By making himself like an object, man acquires a hard crust against which fate comes knocking and bouncing, and an immobility which seems to deprive it of its most redoubtable weapon: time.

It is most significant too that Faulkner retains for all his characters the specifically human privilege of *astonishment*.[28] It is found in a pure form in Anse, who is not only surprised at what happens, but shows surprise at his very surprise:

> He looks around, blinking, in that surprised way, like he had wore hisself down being surprised and was even surprised at that. [p. 31]

The other Bundrens evince the same capacity for wonder. One finds it in Dewey Dell's stupor at her pregnancy, in the helpless bewilderment into which Vardaman is thrown by Addie's death, or again in the expression of "furious incredulity" registered on Jewel's face when the fire occurs (p. 208).

Even among the simplest and most simpleminded, there is this inner distance produced by astonishment which makes a man the incredulous and horrified spectator of his own life:

> It's like there was a fellow in every man that's done a-past the sanity or the insanity, that watches the sane and the insane doings of that man with the same horror and the same astonishment. [p. 228]

Whether their actions are reasonable or not, Faulkner's characters never stop being surprised at what they do or rather at what they are made to do, at what they endure and suffer. Astonishment is always their first reaction to what Faulkner calls *outrage*. This term is, of course, one of the novelist's key words. *As I Lay Dying* is doubtless, along with *Absalom, Absalom!* and *The Wild Palms,* the book in which it recurs most often. The word is used here in two senses—one social, the other moral and metaphysical —which echo each other ironically. Outrage is first a violation of common decency; it is the scandal the Bundrens cause by inflicting the insufferable smell of the corpse on their neighbors. "It's a outrage," cries Rachel Samson (p. 111), and some sixty pages later Lula Armstid expresses her indignation in identical terms (pp. 178–79). But the real outrage, the genuine scandal lies elsewhere: it is in everything that humiliates and crushes man, in all the violence which fate makes him suffer. Its most visible manifestation in the novel is the series of catastrophes which shower down on the Bundrens in the course of their journey, and first of all the rain so often referred to in the opening sections. This rain is expected by everybody and known to be imminent. Yet when it finally starts to fall, Anse looks thoroughly dumbfounded:

from behind his slack-faced astonishment he muses as though from beyond time, upon the ultimate outrage. [p. 72]

The astonishment provoked by the outrage is not the shock of the unexpected but stupefaction at the occurrence of the inescapable:

again he looks up at the sky with that expression of dumb and brooding outrage and yet of vindication, as though he had expected no less. [p. 73]

Astonishment in Faulkner, then, does not preclude foreknowledge. Anse "expected no less"; he knows that what happens was due to happen. The event confirms his expectation, and his outraged air suggests an uncanny wisdom beyond thought:

his humped silhouette partaking of that owl-like quality of awryfeathered, disgruntled outrage within which lurks a wisdom too profound or too inert for even thought [p. 48]

In Anse, the sense of outrage is absorbed into placid astonishment, and astonishment into inertia. The scandal is recognized, but immediately accepted as inevitable. The same is not true of the other Bundrens. Contrary to Anse's, their astonishment indicates (as does *étonnement* in seventeenth-century French tragedy) violent emotion, an upheaval of their whole being. Far from being the furtive blinking of a sleepy consciousness, a kind of unspoken complicity with the irremediable, it marks for Addie the beginning of indignation, it is the first seed of revolt. Thus, when she realizes that she is pregnant for the second time:

At first I would not believe it. Then I believed I would kill Anse. [p. 164]

From disbelief Addie passes straight to rage and hatred. Her astonishment is not dulled into lethargic resignation, but directly provokes her proud will to ripost: it is in order to avenge the outrage to her "aloneness" that Addie makes her husband promise to go and bury her in Jefferson when she is dead. Her funeral journey is, as it were, a last revenge against fate.

Addie bequeathed this refusal to submit to all her children except Darl. Caught in the same trap as her mother, Dewey Dell similarly rebels against what happens to her and, through her efforts to have an abortion, likewise attempts to escape her destiny. Vardaman too refuses to give in to events, and, through the exorcisms of his private magic, busies himself effacing the outrage inflicted on him by his mother's death. Jewel's astonishment instantly flares up into fury—the fury in which he finds the energy of his heroism. Darl's, on the contrary, failing to find release in action or be deadened in inertia, endlessly turns on itself in tortured speculation and is eventually aggravated into madness. Darl is the perfect example of the outraged onlooker of whom Cash speaks at the end of the novel; he is indeed only that: a fascinated and impotent stare, succumbing to the horror of what it sees.

Astonishment at outrage is the encounter of innocence and evil. Whether paralyzed by stupor or driven to fruitless rebellion, Faulkner's characters are above all victims. An obscure curse seems to weigh on them, but they are not guilty. To explain their misfortunes, one could no doubt look for those responsible and incriminate Addie's destructive pride or Anse's massive egoism. But in fact, as Faulkner himself has pointed out,[29] there is no villain in the story other than the absurd convention which makes the Bundrens drag the corpse as far as Jefferson and all the evil forces let loose against them during their agonizing journey. Evil here is on the world's side. It is also *within* man, but it does not spring *from* man. In *As I Lay Dying,* Faulkner's pessimism—insofar as such a label can be used to define his tragicomic vision—is less moral than metaphysical. The themes of sin and guilt appear only marginally, and the historical, social, and racial context of the South in which these themes are treated in most of the novelist's other works is hardly perceptible here. *As I Lay Dying* is an almost timeless fable. The human beings it presents seem to date from before history; yet they have already been exiled from Paradise, and are already doomed and damned. The effects of the primal curse are indeed strongly felt, but Faulkner does not here, as in his other novels, raise questions about the origins of the malediction. What we are shown instead is the naked scandal of existence revealed through the extremes of madness and death. The decomposing corpse dragged along the road is the *memento mori,* a grim reminder of the radically contingent and irremediably finite nature of man; death is, as Addie soon learned, what invalidates all life. As for madness, the other aspect of the scandal, it designates here—like Benjy's idiocy in *The Sound and the Fury*—the intolerable paradox of utter degradation linked to absolute innocence.

Faulkner, too, it seems, is astonished at the scandal of this "terrible" life, and his novel echoes this astonishment very closely. Speculative thinking no doubt also proceeds from wonder but soon goes beyond it; in its desire to make sense of nonsense, it is always at pains to play down absurdity and explain away what appears scandalous to the spontaneous mind, and in the systems it erects, scandal is never more than a moment or an element in the universal order. Nothing like that happens here: Faulkner stubbornly refuses to go beyond astonishment, refuses to question it or to convert it into rational thought; he is content to record that initial moment when a consciousness runs into the intolerable and experiences the shock of outrage. No lesson is drawn, no wisdom offered. Therefore *As I Lay Dying,* which is perhaps the most purely metaphysical of Faulkner's novels, is probably also his least philosophical.

THE LURES AND POWERS OF LANGUAGE

FAR from being, as has sometimes been suggested, a meditation on the human predicament, this novel represents it in its immediate incongruity. It presents it as a spectacle. It says nothing; it *shows.* As Calvin Bedient writes: "*As I Lay Dying* is to be

'seen,' not understood; experienced, not translated; felt, not analyzed."[30] And the same critic asks:

> Is there, indeed, an organizer behind the spectacle? The novel
> does not help us to an answer. What it unfolds before us is simply
> the autonomy of misfortune: the brutal fact of its monotonous
> regularity and astonishing variety, of its farcical absurdity, of its
> tragedy; and questions of cause are not raised—they are extra-
> neous. There is thus in the novel a fundamental silence that is
> truly terrible. For what is more mysterious, finally, than immediacy?
> Explanations tranquilize wonder, and *As I Lay Dying* contains no
> explanations.[31]

Behind this enigmatic spectacle, there is nevertheless an organ-
izer, who is none other than the novelist himself. *As I Lay Dying*
is not life as lived but life as written, contained within the pages
of a book, and the spectacle is made with words.

But are words capable of recreating the felt quality of experience and expressing it with entire truthfulness? Is it possible
to bridge the distance between reality and language?[32] The question is central to the novel: it is Addie who puts it in her monologue, and her answer is a final no:

> I would think how words go straight up in a thin line, quick and
> harmless, and how terribly doing goes along the earth, clinging to
> it, so that after a while the two lines are too far apart for the same
> person to straddle from one to the other. [p. 165]

Verticality and horizontality, air and earth, lightness and weight,
all the contrasts denote here the unbridgeable gap between language and experience. Words have no weight; they fly up and
vanish into thin air, as light as children's balloons. Real life, according to Addie, requires passionate personal commitment, and
its truth can only be reached through actions faithful to the earth
and blood. This antagonism between the reality of life and the
unreality of words is dramatized in the novel by the opposition
of two types of people: the doers (Addie, Cash, Jewel) and the
talkers (Anse, Cora, Whitfield). For the latter group, speech is

a mere mask and sham; the words they use are not the expression of any reality, but its substitute; they do not translate an experience, they take its place. What Anse calls "love" is only the lack of love, "just a shape to fill a lack" (p. 164). Addie's bitter discovery on her first pregnancy is that language is totally inadequate for expression of truth and that its main purpose is to deceive:

> I learned that words are no good; that words dont ever fit even what they are trying to say at. When he was born I knew that motherhood was invented by someone who had to have a word for it because the ones that had the children didn't care whether there was a word for it or not. I knew that fear was invented by someone that had never had fear; pride, who never had the pride. [pp. 163–64]

When she is with child for the second time, however, Addie discovers something else. She then realizes that the seemingly harmless vacuity of words hides formidable powers. Words are traps laid for our weakness, and Addie's rage comes from allowing herself to be caught in them:

> It was as though [Anse] had tricked me, hidden within a word like within a paper screen and struck me in the back through it. [p. 164]

Yet although her resentment is first directed at her husband, Addie soon realizes he has been taken in like herself:

> I realised that I had been tricked by words older than Anse or love, and that the same word had tricked Anse too. . . . [p. 164]

If Addie begins by denouncing the futility of words, experience eventually teaches her to acknowledge their power. Men think they use language for their own purposes, but in fact it is language that uses them and makes game of them, urging them to act in ways they never intended. As a character in *Mosquitoes* points out, the human being belongs to "that species all of whose actions are controlled by words."[33] *As I Lay Dying* is another ironical illustration of this theme: does the whole action of the novel not stem from the *word* given Addie by Anse (cf. pp. 108–109)? While being extraneous to action and experience, language is instrumental in determining them. For whoever seeks in it the locus of truth, there can only be the disappointment of finding an empty shell. Yet in its very emptiness it exerts a coercive power from which none may escape. Man is born into language, just as he is born into time and mortality, and language is part of the intricate network of necessities that subject him to their law; it is one of the many impersonal forces which are shaping his life and, as such, it is just another face of his destiny.

Clearly, then, the relationships between words and things, between language and experience cannot be reduced to a straightforward opposition. And it is also important not to confuse Addie's diatribe against words with the author's position. Addie has a personal account to settle: she indicts language because she began by trusting it and her naive confidence has been betrayed. Moreover, reading her monologue, one retains a suspicion that she continues to believe in it, so ardently does she try to justify herself in words. Ironies like this should put us on our guard against a hasty interpretation of Faulkner's own attitude towards language. No doubt he shared Addie's revulsion to some extent. The futility of words is often proclaimed in his work, and already in *Mosquitoes* we find this revealing remark: "Talk, talk, talk; the utter and heart-breaking stupidity of words."[34] Yet for Faulkner language is also

> that meager and fragile thread . . . by which the little surface corners and edges of men's secret and solitary lives may be joined for an instant now and then before sinking back into the darkness where the spirit cried for the first time and was not heard and will cry for the last time and will not be heard then either.[35]

However tenuous the thread may be, language also possesses the power to bind. If more often than not it is mere deceit and trickery, it does not exclude the possibility of communication, fragile and ephemeral no doubt, but real nonetheless. And if it can never be more than a poor substitute for experience, it can be used in such a way as to capture at least some fragments of its truth. Faulkner's creation is a wager on these possibilities, and has all the anxiety and uncertainty of a wager. It is the novelist's ever-renewed attempt to reconcile experience with form, life with art—an attempt apparently as hopeless as his characters' desperate endeavors to accord consciousness and identity; it is his unflagging effort to build the reality of his work on the unreality of words, and the "splendid failure" which sometimes crowns this effort. What prompts him into this venture is the recognition that immersion into experience, although indispensable, is not enough and that truth becomes man's possession only after what he has lived, felt, and suffered has been transmuted into awareness, recorded by memory, and reordered by imagination. According to Faulkner, this is precisely the task of the novelist: to lend his voice to "the old verities and truths of the heart,"[36] to embody them in a language that respects their rootedness in experience and never yields to the glibness of abstraction. Faulkner's ambition therefore was not so much to "purify the dialect of the tribe" as to thicken its substance, to convert the transparency of its arbitrary signs into the opacity of things and to create a universe of words which would match the real one in its living, teeming density. Hence Faulkner's "furious attitudes," like those of a craftsman frustrated by some intractable material, and all the demon-driven rage and violence that make him twist and torture language to force it into compliance with his impossible "dream."

8

Critical Reception

ALTHOUGH THE EARLY REVIEWS of *As I Lay Dying* hardly warrant prolonged attention as criticism, they are worth considering as an illustration of the prejudices, misconceptions, and sheer blindness which characterized most of the first public responses to Faulkner's work. By and large the novels he published in the thirties were received very cautiously if not with downright hostility. Traditional humanists and social-minded leftists alike took Faulkner to task for indulging in "the cult of cruelty"[1] and wallowing in obscenity, violence, and horror with utter disregard for current standards of taste and morality. There was much annoyance too over the obscurities of his style and the complexities of his narrative method, the young novelist's formal refinements and technical experiments appearing to many reviewers even less justified because his subject matter seemed to derive from the most sordid brand of naturalism.[2]

Both these grievances are found in the reviews of *As I Lay Dying*. Thus for Granville Hicks[3] the two characteristics of the novelist are "his preoccupation with unpleasant subjects and his experimental approach to the novel as a form;" Hicks certainly allows Faulkner some measure of ability, but wonders whether it is not misused for mere acrobatics: "Have we here some new, some sharply individual view of life creating for itself new forms, or a keen but mechanical intelligence posing for itself problems that it loves to solve?" Hence the suspicion that Faulkner's narrative perversity is nothing but a gratuitous game, "a game in which he displays tremendous ingenuity and gives pleasure to the reader by stimulating a like ingenuity on his part." Hicks even suspects Faulkner of "inventing his stories in the regular chronological order and recasting them in some distorted form."

Reservations of the same type appear in other critics. There is generally a kind of puzzled admission of Faulkner's talent, but very little sympathy and understanding for his aims and methods as a writer. Few are willing to accept Faulkner on his own terms. The anonymous reviewer of *As I Lay Dying* in *The New York Times Book Review*[4] writes:

> One . . . feels that one must immediately sit down to write an essay on the province and limitations of fiction. The quality of Mr. Faulkner's own mind, even when it is latent, is of a high order; the quality of the minds of the people he chooses to set before you, in fluid Joycean terms, is, on the contrary, of a very low sort.

And he regrets that Faulkner is not Dostoevski: "He makes us yearn for a Dostoevski to rescue the stream of consciousness and so put it into literary channels whereby it can be handled by the human intellect."

As for Clifton Fadiman,[5] one of the most malevolent and obstinate of Faulkner's denigrators, he sees in the novel nothing but a pointlessly complicated melodrama:

> In his fourth novel Mr. Faulker has to an extent departed from the irritating obscurity which marked *The Sound and the Fury*. It still seems that his is a far more involved technique than his material requires; impudent analysis might reduce this story to the dimensions of simple melodrama.

Fadiman is also irritated by Faulkner's "romantic obsessions," by his interest in abnormal behavior and emotional extremes, and has strong doubts about the objectivity of his characterization: "He seems acute in his portrayal of defective mentalities—but how, really, can one check up on this portrayal?" Yet, although he finds it "difficult to believe him an important writer," Fadiman eventually recognizes the originality of Faulkner's vision: "His cosmos is awry; but it is his own, self-created."

Not all the reviews, however, were as disparaging. In *The New Republic* Kenneth White[6] expressed admiration for "the ingenuity Mr. Faulkner displays in keeping the various strands tightly knit and in contriving the steadily increasing horror," and conceded that "the style, save for occasional passages of meaningless word juggling, is well adapted to the material" and that "the colloquial idiom these farmers speak is excellently handled." *"As I Lay Dying,"* he concluded, "does not offer a pleasant or inspiring view of humanity, but it is an uncommonly forceful book."

It should be remembered, too, that while in the Northern press the critical reception was in most cases indifferent or adverse, there were a handful of critics in the South who gave Faulkner all the attention he deserved. Thus one of the most laudatory reviews of *As I Lay Dying* appeared in the *Times-Picayune,* the New Orleans paper to whose Sunday magazine section Faulkner had contributed sixteen stories and sketches in 1925.[7] According to the reviewer of the *Times-Picayune, As I Lay Dying* has "an integrity of conception and firmness of handling that makes it a distinctive and noteworthy work" although it lacks "the intensity and driving power" of *The Sound and the Fury.* The reviewer was well aware that Faulkner's novel would "scandalize" the "squeamish," but was confident that it would please "those who respect life well interpreted in fine fiction without attempting to dictate what subjects an author shall choose."[8]

In Great Britain, where *As I Lay Dying* was published in September 1935, most critics followed the general American trend, and the way in which they treated Faulkner was even more patronizing than it had been in the United States.[9] Many reviews of the novel betray hasty reading and contain errors about the

plot and characters; although one finds again some reluctant ad-
missions of Faulkner's talent, there is no serious attempt at objective analysis and assessment of his work. For most British
reviewers Faulkner is simply a painter of low life with morbid
tastes, and the wry humor of his book passes totally unnoticed.
In *The Listener,* Edwin Muir[10] accused him of indulging in his
necrophilic obsessions and, like many others, objected to the
complexity of his technique. In the tragicomic adventures of the
Bundrens, Muir found little to praise; the macabre story of
Addie's corpse made his Victorian stomach heave: "the effect is
not horror but merely disgust." Howard Spring,[11] the reviewer
of the *Evening Standard,* was no gentler: he qualified the book as
"affected and annoying" and, echoing a familiar complaint, censured Faulkner for translating his characters' thought processes
into his own words and thus disregarding the demands of realism.

A year after the first English edition, Philip Henderson, in
The Novel Today: Studies in Contemporary Attitudes,[12] gave
a general assessment of Faulkner's work. We shall quote him at
some length because his point of view illustrates with comic perfection the shortsightedness of the leftist critics in the thirties.
To Faulkner's greater confusion, Henderson contrasts his supposed lack of social conscience and grimacing nihilism with Caldwell's "constructive" realism:

> Erskine Caldwell's *Tobacco Road* also deals with "poor whites"
> who have been reduced to an almost sub-human condition by the
> stagnation of agriculture in the southern states. But Caldwell not
> only gives an unforgettable picture of this world in all the bitter
> humour of its ruin, but, by his concrete social setting, shows us why
> his agricultural morons are as they are and indicates how their in-
> dividual helplessness can be remedied by large-scale collective
> farming on the part of both whites and blacks. Compared to Cald-
> well's realistic pages, . . . Faulkner's human wrecks are but the
> twisted shapes of his own despair.

[*141*

In France *As I Lay Dying* fared much better. Published by Gallimard in 1934,[13] the novel was doubly favored by the excellent translation by Maurice Edgar Coindreau—who three years before had already hailed Faulkner as "one of the most interesting figures in recent American letters"[14] and by Valéry Larbaud's preface. Contrary to most American and British reviewers, the French novelist promptly recognized the merits of the book:

> *As I Lay Dying* undoubtedly offers more interest and, in my opinion, has a far higher aesthetic quality than the vast majority of books it has to be shelved with in bookshops for the convenience of the public, that is to say under the label "rustic novel."[15]

Larbaud was the first to notice the book's affinities with the theater, and his suggestive comparison of Addie's burial with the obsequies of a Homeric queen also called attention to the epic quality of the novel:

> We can, without any question of making a parody on the novel, transpose it into an episode of epic dimensions: the episode of the funeral procession of the (Homeric) queen, Addie Bundren, conducted, in accordance with her final wishes, by her husband, Anse, and by her children, the princes.[16]

The French press took its cue from Larbaud's preface: most reviewers also emphasized the epic character of *As I Lay Dying*. There were no doubt some reservations; Marcel Thiébaut found Faulkner's style "too consciously literary"[17] on occasion, and Eugène Dabit thought that his art sometimes lacked simplicity.[18] But there was neither petty quibbling nor queasy condescension. Praise won the day: the French critics were all impressed by Faulkner's skillful use of the interior monologue and they were more or less unanimous in finding the book to have "the sweep of a great lyric fresco."[19] Dabit, who had just tried his own hand at the same subject in *Un Mort tout neuf,* envied the scope of Faulkner's vision:

I saw an amplification of my own adventure. It unfolded within another frame, broader and wild, under a real sky, in the torrid heat of the South; the characters that interested me were weighty, [obstinate, bizarre,] dominated by their destiny, submissive to primitive instincts which are not those of the petty French bourgeois.[20]

Further on he added these perceptive remarks on Faulkner's realism:

This realism is pitiless, violent, on a large scale, occasionally comical, with deep blacks, sulphurous yellows, bright reds. Its main object is to present men in their daily existence, to tell us of their work, to show us their defects and their passions. But all this is offered pell-mell, in a way which cannot but surprise us, with outbursts of lyricism, punctuated with accents of grating irony, with nothing attenuated, soft-pedaled or polished. It appears that one of the preoccupations of William Faulkner is to present us tragedies in the raw, without preparation, to use his characters somewhat as symbols and to give his landscape, smells and lights the same importance as his characters, everything being blended and interwoven.[21]

It is worth recalling too that Paris saw the first adaptation of *As I Lay Dying* for the stage thanks to Jean-Louis Barrault.[22] For the young actor, then an extra with Charles Dullin, the novel was a revelation:[23] he strove for months to turn it into a sort of pantomime and, in June 1935, finally presented his show, never since revived, under the title *Autour d'une mère*. The performances were given at the Théâtre de l'Atelier with settings and costumes by the surrealist painter Felix Labisse. The production, known only through Antonin Artaud's writings[24] besides Barrault's own, appears to have been an experiment in antirealistic theater, an attempt to re-create drama in its magic and ritual forms; in Barrault's own words, it was "drama in its primitive state,"[25] based essentially on bodily expression, with two short expository scenes and two lyrical monologues by the mother as the only text. Barrault had been particularly interested in Jewel's dealings with his horse, and this provided a good deal of material for mime, but he also played the role of the mother and made her a sort of idol or totem, impersonating her stripped to the waist over a flared skirt, wearing a mask and an enormous black wig.

With the French public, *As I Lay Dying,* like the other novels by Faulkner translated around that time, soon won fervent admirers, and in an interview published in 1950,[26] Barrault declared that Faulkner was one of the writers who had had the greatest influence on his generation. In the United States it took him longer to gain recognition and it was only from the forties onwards that his work began to be taken seriously. The reaction was predictable: in order to clear the novelist of the charge of nihilism and amorality, he was speedily awarded the white badge of humanism. Thus George Marion O'Donnell, in an essay published in 1939, presented Faulkner as a "traditional moralist, in the best sense."[27] In his view, *As I Lay Dying* is above all a legend and an allegory: "the procession of ragged, depraved hillmen, carrying Addie Bundren's body through water and through fire to the cemetery in Jefferson, while people flee from the smell and buzzards circle overhead—this progress is not unlike that of the medieval soul toward redemption."[28] From being degenerate and debased clodhoppers, the heroes of the novel are now hailed as champions of morality: "the Bundrens are able to carry a genuine act of traditional morality through to its end."[29] O'Donnell's essay established a pattern of interpretation followed by many subsequent commentators. Robert Penn Warren, for example, holds the same point of view; "the whole of *As I Lay Dying,*" he asserts, "is based on the heroic effort of the Bundren family to fulfill the promise to the dead mother."[30] In his remarkable study of the Yoknapatawpha County novels, Cleanth Brooks also makes much of the Bundrens' heroism. While showing more subtlety and circumspection than Warren or O'Donnell, he does not exclude the possibility that "one of Faulkner's principal themes—perhaps the principal theme—is the nature of the heroic deed."[31] According to Brooks, the concern for family honor evinced by these poor whites is just as demanding and punctilious as the code of Faulkner's aristocrats and accounts for much of their quixotic behavior.[32] He concludes that

> As a commentary upon man's power to act and to endure, upon his apparently incorrigible idealism, the story of the Bundrens is clearly appalling—appalling but not scathing and not debunking. Heroism is heroism even though it sometimes appears to be merely the hither side of folly. . . . For a summarizing statement on *As I Lay Dying,* one might appeal to one of the choruses in *Antigone:* "Wonders are many, and none is more wonderful than man." *As I Lay Dying* provides a less exalted but not unworthy illustration of Sophocles' judgment.[33]

Among the humanist interpretations of the novel one could also count Irving Howe's. "Of all Faulkner's novels," he writes, "*As I Lay Dying* is the warmest, the kindliest and most affectionate."[34] Howe's emphasis is not so much on the heroism of the Bundrens; what strikes him most is the writer's profound sympathy for his characters:

> In no other work is he so receptive to people, so ready to take and love them. . . . Look—he seems to be saying—look at the capacity for suffering and dignity which human beings have, even the most absurdly wretched of them! The book is a triumph of fraternal feeling. . . ."[35]

Melvin Backman's reading of the novel is very similar to Howe's in its conclusions:

> As in *The Sound and the Fury* Faulkner told the story of a family, but the Bundren family, despite its losses and troubles, is rooted in the earth and life. *As I Lay Dying* is a story about people; it is a fable and poem which is simply and joyously alive. Anguish gives way to comedy, despair to duty, inversion to action, and obsession to love."[36]

Finally, in a more recent book, Walter Brylowski contrasts the "dark vision" of *The Sound and the Fury* with the "comic vision" of *As I Lay Dying,* which is, in his opinion, "an affirmation of life in the face of death and the forces of nature which deal out both life and death."[37]

In her influential essay on the novel, first published in 1950,[38] Olga W. Vickery had suggested a far less optimistic interpretation. More concerned with the implications of structure and technique than with easy philosophical generalizations, she analyzed *As I Lay Dying* primarily as a study of family tension, and her interest in the variety of individual responses to the central event of Addie's death made her more sensitive than most other critics to the complexities and ambiguities of the novel. Yet on one point at least she was perfectly clear: far from interpreting the Bundrens' funeral journey as a heroic act of traditional morality, she considered it as "a travesty of the ritual of interment"[39] from beginning to end.

Other critics were to go much further in their rejection of the heroic and optimistic interpretation that had won general acceptance during the fifties. The most vehement among them was undoubtedly Edward Wasiolek.[40] Questioning the critical consensus, he strongly emphasizes the incongruous and horrible aspects of the journey as well as the stupid selfishness of most of the Bundrens, and is at pains to show that the relationship between Faulkner and his characters is neither tragic identification nor comic distance. In his view, what predominates in the novel is satire and irony:

> Faulkner's tone is bitterly ironic, resigned, and masochistically insistent not only on the bitter condition of man's life, but also on obtuseness of man's awareness of it. The "humor" of *As I Lay Dying* grimaces grotesquely through the doomed protest of Addie and Faulkner against the condition of isolation which all men share and against the insensitivity of most to that isolation.[41]

This conception of the novel comes close to that of Edward L. Volpe, for whom *As I Lay Dying* is above all a masterpiece of black humor. "His short novel," Volpe writes, "presents human existence as an absurd joke,"[42] and further on he draws this revealing Swiftian analogy: "Reading about the Bundrens is somewhat like watching monkeys; we identify with the lower primates in the zoo enough to make us simultaneously amused and uncomfortable."[43]

Must we then choose between the humanists and the "absurdists"? As was suggested in the introductory chapter, these mutually exclusive views of *As I Lay Dying* are equally limiting and proceed from the same disregard for the essential openness of the novel's form and meaning. It is as arbitrary to raise the book to epic heights as to reduce it to a macabre joke, as false to see in it a joyful affirmation of life as to read it as a profession of nihilism. The sense of the absurd is obviously there, and it is conveyed to us through Addie and especially through Darl, whom the novelist has made his principal narrator. But Darl, whatever his secret links with the author may be, is not Faulkner, and no one is the novelist's mandated spokesman.

To discover what Faulkner thought about this novel, one may consult the record of his interviews. Considering his remarks on *As I Lay Dying,* the reader is tempted to decide in favor of the humanists' interpretation: Faulkner by no means decried his characters, regarded them neither as primates nor as monsters, and even Anse[44] and Whitfield[45] are forgiven by their merciful creator. For Faulkner, the Bundrens are above all victims; yet he also ranks them with those, such as Lena Grove, who could face up to their destinies and were able to endure: "The Bundren family in *As I Lay Dying* pretty well coped with their fate."[46]

Critics, of course, cannot afford to ignore the author's remarks, but it would be utterly naive to consider Faulkner as an infallible authority on his work and to expect from him final revelations on its meaning. His comments sometimes lead us to the threshold of his workshop, never further; they throw light on the novelist's intentions, but between these and the completed novels are all the additional significances, produced by the creative process itself, which lend each work its particular density. It is just that tangled mass of meaning, coextensive with the unique form of each book and consequently irreducible to the humanist or antihumanist ideologies to which it has been attached, that critics of Faulkner now need to explore and bring to light.

NOTES

1. Introduction

1. *Lion in the Garden: Interviews with William Faulkner, 1926–1962,* ed. James B. Meriwether and Michael Millgate (New York: Random House, 1968), p. 220. This work will be referred to hereafter as *LG.*

2. See James M. Mellard, "Faulkner's Philosophical Novel: Ontological Themes in *As I Lay Dying," The Personalist,* XLVIII (Autumn 1967), 509–23.

3. For a fuller discussion of the critical responses to the novel, see chapter 8.

4. See Walter Brylowski, *Faulkner's Olympian Laugh* (Detroit: Wayne State University Press, 1968), p. 86.

5. *Faulkner in the University: Class Conferences at the University of Virginia, 1957–1958,* ed. Frederick L. Gwynn and Joseph L. Blotner (Charlottesville: University of Virginia Press, 1959), p. 87; referred to hereafter as *FU.* See also *LG,* pp. 222, 244.

6. In this connection, it is interesting to note that Faulkner may have borrowed the title of his novel from one of the English translations of *The Odyssey.* See Carvel Collins, "The Pairing of *The Sound and the Fury* and *As I Lay Dying," Princeton University Library Chronicle,* XVIII (Spring 1957), 123.

7. See Richard Chase, *The American Novel and Its Tradition* (New York: Doubleday Anchor Books, 1957), pp. 1–28.

8. Calvin Bedient, "Pride and Nakedness: *As I Lay Dying," Modern Language Quarterly,* XXIX (March 1968), 61.

9. See *FU,* pp. 87, 113, 207; *LG,* pp. 180, 222, 244.

10. See *FU,* p. 61.

11. According to the first interviews with Faulkner, published in 1931 and 1932, for some time the author considered *As I Lay Dying* his best novel (see *LG,* pp. 8, 13, 32). But later his preference went to *The Sound and the Fury.*

2. Genesis and Sources

1. Introduction to *Sanctuary* (New York: Modern Library, 1932), p. vii.

2. See *FU*, pp. 87, 207; *LG*, p. 180.

3. The manuscript and carbon typescript are in the Alderman Library of the University of Virginia; the typescript setting copy is at the University of Texas. The first page of the manuscript was reproduced in Jean Stein, "William Faulkner," *The Paris Review*, IV (Spring 1956), 32–33. The last page was reproduced in *The Princeton University Library Chronicle*, XVIII (Spring 1957), as illustration V, pp. 128 ff.

4. See George Palmer Garrett, "Some Revisions in *As I Lay Dying*," *Modern Language Notes*, LXXIII (June 1958), 414–17.

5. *Mosquitoes* (New York: Liveright, 1927), p. 340.

6. Both changes are also thematically significant: "box," being more indeterminate than "coffin," surreptitiously paves the way for the ambiguous symbolism associated with Addie's death; at the same time its undignified banality suggests the anonymity of death and the objectlike condition of the corpse. "Addie Bundren" instead of "Maw" indicates from the outset Darl's estrangement from his mother.

7. Paul Verlaine, *Oeuvres Poétiques Complètes* (Paris: Gallimard, 1948), p. 206: "où l'Indécis au Précis se joint."

8. See James A. Winn, "Faulkner's Revisions: A Stylist at Work," *American Literature*, XLI (May 1969), 231–50.

9. *LG*, p. 244.

10. See Michael Millgate, *The Achievement of William Faulkner* (New York: Random House, 1966), p. 26. The text quoted by Millgate is probably an unpublished introduction Faulkner wrote for *The Sound and the Fury*.

11. Joseph L. Fant and Robert Ashley, eds., *Faulkner at West Point* (New York: Random House, 1964), pp. 96–97.

12. *LG*, p. 255.

13. Reprinted in *New Orleans Sketches*, edited and introduced by Carvel Collins (New Brunswick, N.J.: Rutgers University Press, 1958), pp. 169–84. Among the early sketches foreshadowing *As I Lay Dying*, Collins also mentions "Yo Ho and Two Bottles of Rum," a story in which the corpse of a Chinese cabin boy is carted under the

blazing sun. Some aspects of the novel are adumbrated as well in "Adolescence," an unpublished story written in the early twenties, and "Elmer," a novel Faulkner had begun during his trip abroad in 1925 but never finished. The young heroine's name in the first story is Juliet Bunden; her mother, now dead, was a schoolteacher with romantic ideas not unlike Addie, and her stepmother, a "tall angular shrew," anticipates the second Mrs. Bundren. There is also a reflection on death which closely parallels Doctor Peabody's (cf. pp. 42–43): "Even dying couldn't help her: death being nothing but that state those left behind are cast into." In "Elmer," the hero's father, described as "that inverted Io with hookworm and a passionate ambitious wife for gadfly" and "too lazy to get bald even," point ahead to Anse, while his mother, an indomitable woman, and Jo-Addie, his equally proud and passionate sister, prefigure Addie Bundren. There is a sentence too which reminds one strongly of the latter's "dying": "His mother's fretful presence seemed yet to linger here like an odor, as though it had not even time for sleep, let alone death." (The typescripts of both stories are in the Alderman Library of the University of Virginia. See James B. Meriwether, *The Literary Career of William Faulkner: A Bibliographical Study* (Princeton University Library, 1961), pp. 13, 81, 86.)

14. See John B. Cullen, "The Yocona River and *As I Lay Dying*" in *Old Times in the Faulkner Country* (Chapel Hill: University of North Carolina Press, 1961), pp. 84–88.

15. See Chapter 4.

16. For a more detailed study of the analogies between Eliot's poem and Faulkner's novel, see Mary Jane Dickerson, *"As I Lay Dying* and The 'Waste Land'—Some Relationships," *Mississippi Quarterly,* XVII (Summer 1964), 129–35.

17. Among those who stress Frazer's influence, see especially Carvel Collins, "The Pairing of *The Sound and the Fury* and *As I Lay Dying,*" *Princeton University Library Chronicle,* XVIII (Spring 1957), 114–23; and Mary Jane Dickerson, "Some Sources of Faulkner's Myth in *As I Lay Dying,*" *Mississippi Quarterly,* XIX (Summer 1966), 132–42.

18. See Walter Brylowski, *Faulkner's Olympian Laugh* (Detroit: Wayne State University Press, 1968), p. 84, note.

19. See Joseph L. Blotner, *"As I Lay Dying:* Christian Lore and Irony," *Twentieth Century Literature,* III (April 1957), 14–19.

20. On the relationship between the two novels, see Harold J.

Douglas and Robert Daniel, "Faulkner and the Puritanism of the South," *Tennessee Studies in Literature*, II (1957), 1–14; and Robert Bridgman, "As Hester Prynne Lay Dying," *English Language Notes*, II (June 1965), 294–96.

21. Like the Tulls, the Armstids, Doctor Peabody, and other minor characters of the novel, Whitfield reappears episodically in several other works. In *The Hamlet* (New York: Random House, 1940) he is described as "a harsh, stupid, honest, superstitious and upright man" (p. 231). In "Shingles for the Lord," a short story first published in 1943, he is presented as the energetic and respected leader of his congregation and shows none of the despicable traits that characterize him in *As I Lay Dying*. Cf. *Collected Stories* (New York: Random House, 1950), pp. 27–43.

22. *FU*, p. 115.

23. Claude Lévi-Strauss, *The Savage Mind*, trans. anon. (Chicago: University of Chicago Press, 1966), p. 17.

3. Language and Style

1. See Faulkner's own comments on these two words in *FU*, p. 126.

2. Florence Leaver, "Faulkner: The Word as Principle and Power," in *Faulkner: Three Decades of Criticism*, ed. Frederick J. Hoffman and Olga W. Vickery (East Lansing: Michigan State University Press, 1960), p. 202.

3. Cf. this reflection of Faulkner on himself and Thomas Wolfe: "We tried to crowd and cram everything, all experience, into each paragraph, to get the whole complete nuance of the moment's experience, of all the recaptured light rays, into each paragraph" (*LG*, p. 107).

4. See Michel Gresset, "Le 'parce que' chez Faulkner et le 'donc' chez Beckett," *Les Lettres Nouvelles*, IX (Nov. 1961), 124–38.

5. Julia Randall, "Some Notes on *As I Lay Dying*," *The Hopkins Review*, IV (Summer 1951), 47.

6. Wright Morris, *The Territory Ahead* (New York: Atheneum, 1963), p. 176.

7. Robert Humphrey, *Stream of Consciousness in the Modern Novel* (Berkeley and Los Angeles: University of California Press, 1954), p. 72.

8. Ibid., pp. 72–73.

9. "Flesh and blood," originally a biblical phrase (it occurs repeatedly in Saint Paul's epistles, denoting human nature in its weakness as opposed to man's spiritual being), is used in similar ways and for similar purposes in *The Sound and the Fury,* where Faulkner also puts it ironically into the mouths of unlikeable characters, e.g. Mrs. Compson.

10. Gustave Flaubert, *Oeuvres complètes* (Paris: Louis Conard, 1910–1954), III, p. 79: "Je suis dévoré de comparaisons, comme on l'est de poux, et je ne passe mon temps qu'à les écraser; mes phrases en grouillent."

4. Technique

1. On the symbolism of the journey, see chapter 7.

2. Cleanth Brooks, *William Faulkner: The Yoknapatawpha Country* (New Haven: Yale University Press, 1963), p. 145.

3. Henry James, *The Art of the Novel: Critical Prefaces,* with an Introduction by Richard P. Blackmur (New York: Charles Scribner's Sons, 1934), p. 110.

4. "Emblem" only partially translates "mise en abyme," retaining its primitive heraldic sense but losing the connotations it has in modern French criticism. André Gide, the first to apply the phrase to literature, used it as a way to define the device of internal reflection in a play or a novel. See his *Journal: 1889–1939* (Paris: Gallimard, Bibliothèque de la Pléiade, 1948), p. 41.—Trans.

5. It is not possible to decide from the text how many days pass between Addie's death and the departure for Jefferson. According to Tull (p. 87) it is three days, whereas for Samson (p. 107), the journey begins three days after the funeral service, namely, four days after her death. On this point, see Edmond L. Volpe, *A Reader's Guide to William Faulkner* (New York: Noonday Press, 1964), p. 379.

6. In section 12 of the manuscript, Faulkner had at first put all the verbs down to the italicized portion in the present tense, then changed his mind and inserted the preterite above the present. Only when typing the text did he opt for the present.

7. Although speeches by absent or dead characters are contrary to

the norms of realistic fiction, they were quite permissible in traditional rhetoric as prosopopeia.

8. According to Julia Randall, "the whole book . . . is something which is being remembered, being sifted, being understood" ("Some Notes on *As I lay Dying*," *The Hopkins Review*, IV, Summer 1951, p. 50). Such a view, however, is invalidated by a close analysis of the novel's technique. To postulate that all the events of the story are past events relived *as if* they were present is a farfetched and rather gratuitous assumption; while explaining away some of the temporal inconsistencies of the novel, it raises many other questions. Some justification for it may no doubt be found in the closing sections (Cash's especially), but the immediacy of the present moment is obviously given greater emphasis in the book than the recollection of the past. On this point, see R. W. Franklin's convincing study of the "Narrative Management in *As I Lay Dying*" in *Modern Fiction Studies*, XIII (Spring 1967), 57–65.

9. See Franklin, 61. The author of this article notes a total of seven anachronistic sections.

10. Cf. Henry James (*Notes on Novelists*): "To lift our subject out of the sphere of anecdote and place it in the sphere of drama . . . we supply it with a large lucid reflector, which we find only . . . in that mind and soul concerned in the business that have at once the highest sensibility and the highest capacity, or that are . . . most admirably agitated." Quoted by Wayne C. Booth in *The Rhetoric of Fiction* (Chicago: University of Chicago Press, 1961), p. 270.

11. The distinction between *history* and *discourse—récit* and *discours* in the original—is taken from Emile Benvéniste. See *Problems in General Linguistics,* trans. Mary Elizabeth Meek (Coral Gables, Fla.: University of Miami Press, 1971), pp. 205–17.

12. As Wayne C. Booth puts it, Faulkner's method in *As I Lay Dying* is "omniscience with teeth in it" (op cit., p. 161).

5. *The Characters*

1. *FU*, p. 47. Cf. pp. 58, 74, 118, 147.

2. See Faulkner's statement in *FU*, p. 118: "I think that any writer worth his salt is convinced that he can create much better people than God can." On Faulkner's kinship with Balzac, see Claude-Edmonde Magny, *L'Age du Roman Americain* (Paris: Editions du Seuil, 1948), pp. 230–43.

3. Jean-Jacques Mayoux, *Vivants Piliers: Le Roman anglo-saxon et les symboles* (Paris: Julliard, 1960), p. 257: "la recherche de l'expressif et du surexpressif." One of Mayoux's very stimulating essays, "The Creation of the Real in William Faulkner," has been translated in *Faulkner: Three Decades of Criticism,* ed. Frederick J. Hoffman and Olga W. Vickery (East Lansing: Michigan State University Press, 1960), pp. 156–73.

4. Mayoux, p. 255: "le langage du corps."

5. See E. M. Forster, *Aspects of the Novel* (Harmondsworth: Penguin Books, 1962), pp. 75–84.

6. Anse reminds one at times of Sut Lovingood, the "natural born durn fool" created by George Washington Harris. See M. Thomas Inge, "William Faulkner and George Washington Harris: In the Tradition of Southwestern humor," *Tennessee Studies in Literature,* VII (1962), 47–59.

7. See Carvel Collins, "The Pairing of *The Sound and the Fury* and *As I Lay Dying,*" *Princeton University Library Chronicle,* XVIII (Spring 1957), 120.

8. See Leslie A. Juhasz, *William Faulkner's As I Lay Dying* (New York: Monarch Press, 1965), pp. 28–29.

9. See Collins, 119–22.

10. Faulkner saw in this similarity the only link between the two novels. Cf. *FU,* p. 207: "If there is any relationship it's probably simply because both of them happened to have a sister in a roaring gang of menfolks."

11. E.g., Temple Drake in *Sanctuary* and Charlotte Rittenmeyer in *The Wild Palms.*

12. In the unpublished introduction to *The Sound and the Fury* quoted by Michael Millgate (*The Achievement of William Faulkner,* New York: Random House, 1966, p. 26), Faulkner writes of Caddy: "So I, who had never had a sister and was fated to lose my daughter in infancy, set out to make myself a beautiful and tragic little girl."

13. Calvin Bedient, "Pride and Nakedness: *As I Lay Dying,*" *Modern Language* Quarterly, XXIX (March 1968), 65.

14. The phrase is from Maurice Le Breton, "Le Thème de la vie et de la mort dans *As I Lay Dying,*" *Revue des Lettres Modernes* (Configuration critique de William Faulkner II), V (Winter 1958–59), 297.

15. See chapter 2.

16. Charles Baudelaire, *Oeuvres complètes* (Paris: Gallimard,

1954), p. 1009: "L'imagination, faculté suprême et tyrannique, sub-stituée au coeur. . . . Energie soudaine d'action, rapidité de décision, fusion mystique du raisonnement et de la passion. . . . Goût immodéré de la séduction, de la domination. . . ."

17. Ibid., p. 1008: "ce bizarre androgyne;" pp. 1008–1009: "elle était presque mâle . . . ;" p. 1009: "elle se donne . . . d'une manière toute masculine, à des drôles qui ne sont pas ses égaux. . . ."

18. Cleanth Brooks, *William Faulkner: The Yoknapatawpha Country* (New Haven: Yale University Press, 1963), p. 148.

19. Addie's sadistic impulses, for example, could be interpreted as masochism in reverse; her own commentary on the whipping scene strongly suggests the ambivalent character of her violence: "When the switch fell I could feel it upon my flesh; when it welted and ridged it was my blood that ran . . ." (p. 162). The whipping scene may be compared with the infantile fantasies Freud analyzed in his essay "A Child is being beaten" (first published in *Zeitschrift,* Bd. V, 1919; reprinted in *Collected Papers,* II, London, 1953, pp. 232–43). According to Freud, these beating fantasies are retained for purposes of autoerotic gratification and go through masochistic as well as sadistic phases; in connection with Addie, it is also interesting to note that for Freud in many cases these fantasies have their origin in an incestuous attachment to the father.

20. Anse's weakness and helplessness are comically emphasized by the fact that he is toothless. In the symbolism of dreams losing one's teeth often represents the fear of castration. In this perspective Anse's journey to Jefferson, where he intends to buy a new set of teeth and get another wife, may be viewed as a parodical reconquest of man-hood, following the matriarchal reign of Addie, the "castrating" wife and mother.

21. Brooks, p. 154.

22. Among the critics who think that Cash undergoes a significant change in the course of the journey, see especially Irving Howe, *William Faulkner,* 2nd edition, rev. (New York: Vintage Books, 1962), p. 188; and Olga W. Vickery, *The Novels of William Faulkner* (Baton Rouge: Louisiana State University Press, 1959), p. 57.

23. *Go Down, Moses* (New York: Random House, 1942), pp. 130–31.

24. A similar situation is found in *Absalom, Absalom!,* where Charles Bon waits just as hopelessly to be recognized by Thomas Sutpen, his father.

25. See these remarks by Jean-Paul Sartre: "This is precisely why the recognition that it is impossible to *possess* an object involves for the for-itself a violent urge to *destroy* it. To destroy is to reabsorb into myself; it is to enter along with the being-in-itself of the destroyed object into a relation as profound as that of creation. . . . Destruction realizes appropriation perhaps more keenly than creation does, for the object destroyed is no longer there to show itself impenetrable" (*Being and Nothingness,* trans. Hazel E. Barnes, New York: Washington Square Press, 1966, pp. 726–27).

26. *FU,* p. 110.

27. On this point, see R. D. Laing, *The Divided Self: An Existential Study in Sanity and Madness* (London: Tavistock Publications, 1959). The case studies of schizoid and schizophrenic patients presented by Laing offer many close similarities with Darl's madness. There could scarcely be better proof of the depth and accuracy of Faulkner's imaginative insight.

28. *The Sound and the Fury* (New York: Jonathan Cape and Harrison Smith, 1929), p. 220.

29. For a sample of misconceptions about Dewey Dell, see Howe, p. 181; Irving Malin, *William Faulkner* (Stanford: Stanford University Press, 1957), p. 46; J. L. Roberts, "The Individual and the Family: Faulkner's *As I Lay Dying,*" *Arizona Quarterly,* XVI (Spring 1960), 28. For a judicious rehabilitation of the character, see Richard J. Stonesifer, "In Defense of Dewey Dell," *Educational Leader,* XXII (July 1, 1958), 27–33.

30. The Mississippi "rednecks" sometimes gave their children the names of governors, senators, and local politicians. Vardaman owes his name to James Kimble Vardaman (1861–1930), a notorious figure in Mississippi politics during the early decades of the twentieth century. See *FU,* p. 115.

31. See especially Harry Modean Campbell, "Experiment and Achievement: *As I Lay Dying* and *The Sound and the Fury,*" *"Sewanee Review,* LI (April 1943), 307; Howe, p. 179; Edward Wasiolek, *"As I Lay Dying:* Distortion in the Slow Eddy of Current Opinion," *Critique,* III (Spring-Fall 1959), 18–22; J. L. Roberts, 30. The notion that Vardaman is an idiot has been refuted by Floyd C. Watkins and William B. Dillingham in "The Mind of Vardaman Bundren," *Philological Quarterly,* XXXIX (April 1960), 247–51.

32. Collins, 121.

33. For a psychoanalytic interpretation of the fish=fetus equation,

see especially Sandor Ferenczi, *Thalassa: A Theory of Genitality* (New York: The Psychoanalytic Quarterly, 1938). Psychoanalysts would probably identify the fish as a penis symbol as well as an image of the child in the womb; Vardaman's fantasy could thus be interpreted as a reference to the primal family trinity and as an expression of the "basic dream" in the sense defined by Norman O. Brown: "The basic dream is of self as embryo in womb = penis in womb = parents in coitus; the primal scene" (*Love's Body,* New York: Vintage Books, 1966, p. 57).

34. As much could be said of the horse symbol connected with Jewel. Although the horse is primarily a mother surrogate, it is also a kind of self-projection. Jewel treats his horse as he was treated by his mother. Moreover, as R. W. Stallman noted, "in addressing the horse as 'sweet son of a bitch,' Jewel is addressing himself, that bastard" ("A Cryptogram: *As I Lay Dying,*" in *The Houses that James Built,* East Lansing: Michigan State University Press, 1961, p. 204).

35. *FU*, p. 111.

6. The Setting

1. *The Wild Palms* (New York: Random House, 1939), p. 138.

2. See John K. Simon, "The Scene and the Imagery of Metamorphosis in *As I Lay Dying,*" *Criticism,* VII (Winter 1965), 1–22. This perceptive and stimulating article—in which I found many useful suggestions for my own study—was the first to deal extensively with the *scene* of the novel and to stress the significance of Faulkner's apocalyptic imagery.

3. *LG*, p. 253.

4. Similarly lyrical descriptions of horses are found in *Sartoris* (New York: Harcourt, Brace and Company, 1929), pp. 130, 132, and in an early story, "Carcassonne," originally published in *These Thirteen* (New York: Jonathan Cape and Harrison Smith, 1931), pp. 352–58, and reprinted in *Collected Stories of William Faulkner* (New York: Random House, 1950), pp. 895–900. See also the "spotted horses" episode in *The Hamlet* (New York: Random House, 1940), pp. 309–79. In this connection, it is worth noting that Jewel's horse is a descendant of the wild Texas ponies brought into the county twenty-five years before by Flem Snopes.

5. See Karl E. Zink, "Flux and the Frozen Moment: The Imagery of Stasis in Faulkner's Prose," *PMLA*, LXXI (June 1956), 285–301.

6. The concept of time underlying this passage is extremely ambiguous. While "an irrevocable quality" implies irreversible, linear, historical time, in which things never happen twice, the image of the looping string, like that of the spool (cf. p. 38), suggests circularity, i.e., a cyclic, repetitive, mythical time. Moreover, the river, a symbol of the flow of time, intersects at right angles the direction followed by the Bundrens, as though cosmic and human time were at odds.

7. See chapter 5.

8. Cf. *Soldiers' Pay* (New York: Liveright, 1926), p. 151: "Leaves were like a green liquid arrested in mid-flow, flattened and spread; leaves were as though cut with scissors from green paper and pasted flat on the afternoon."

9. See chapter 5.

7. Themes

1. The tense of the verb underscores the ambiguity, since "lay," normally the past tense, is used as the present in the spoken language of the novel itself.

2. See chapter 1.

3. See chapter 6.

4. The twilight motif appears very early in Faulkner's work and is charged from the beginning with symbolic connotations. On this point, see Michael Millgate, *The Achievement of William Faulkner* (New York: Random House, 1966), p. 86; and Richard P. Adams, *Faulkner: Myth and Motion* (Princeton, N.J.: Princeton University Press, 1968), pp. 26–27.

5. Maurice Blanchot, *L'Espace Littéraire* (Paris: Gallimard, 1968; first edition, 1955), p. 351: "le cadavre est sa propre image."

6. On the motif of the unburiable cadaver, see John K. Simon, "The Scene and the Imagery of Metamorphosis in *As I Lay Dying*," 1–22, especially 13 ff.; and J. Russell Reaver, "This Vessel of Clay: A Thematic Comparison of Faulkner's *As I Lay Dying* and Latorre's *The Old Woman of Peralillo*," *Arizona Quarterly*, XVI (Spring 1960), 26–38.

7. On this point, see Lucien Lévy-Bruhl, *Primitive Mentality*,

trans. Lillian A. Clare (New York: Macmillan, 1923), pp. 59–96, especially pp. 68–69.

8. Edgar Morin, *L'Homme et la Mort* (Paris: Corréa, 1951), p. 99: "toute mort est analogue à un changement de naissance, toute naissance est analogue à un changement de mort, tout changement est analogue à une mort-renaissance—et le cycle de la vie humaine est analogue aux cycles naturels de mort-renaissance."

9. The association of death and motherhood is also suggested by the symbolism of the buzzards. In addition to being death symbols, vultures are often linked with fecundity in folklore and myth. In many African and American myths, the vulture is equated with a pregnant woman: Nekhbet, the Egyptian vulture-goddess was the goddess of births. In psychoanalysis too, the vulture has been interpreted as a mother symbol. See, e.g., S. Freud, *Leonardo da Vinci: A Study in Psychosexuality* (New York: Random House, 1947).

10. Throughout Faulkner's fiction, the tree appears as a symbol of femininity and fecundity. See, for example, *Soldiers' Pay*, p. 44: "impervious trees occupied solely with maternity and spring." It is also interesting to note that in "Old Man" the convict discovers the pregnant woman in a tree (*The Wild Palms*, New York: Random House, 1939, p. 148).

11. Darl's apocalyptic vision is foreshadowed in *Sartoris*: "the sun that spread like a crimson egg broken on the ultimate hills" (p. 306).

12. Vardaman explicitly likens Addie's death to a journey (see p. 63).

13. Hyatt H. Waggoner, *William Faulkner: From Jefferson to the World* (Lexington: University of Kentucky Press, 1959), p. 62.

14. On the symbolism of the coffin, see R. W. Stallman, "A Cryptogram: *As I Lay Dying*," in *The Houses that James Built* (East Lansing: Michigan State University Press, 1961), pp. 209–210.

15. Rabi, "Faulkner and the Exiled Generation," in *Faulkner: Two Decades of Criticism*, ed. Frederick J. Hoffman and Olga W. Vickery (East Lansing: Michigan State College Press, 1951), p. 129. Translated from "Faulkner et la génération de l'exil," *Esprit*, XIX (January 1951), 56.

16. The phrase is from Gaston Bachelard, *L'Eau et les Rêves* (Paris: José Corti, 1942), p. 111: "les quatre patries de la mort."

17. Mircea Eliade, *Birth and Rebirth* (New York: Harper and

Brothers, 1958). See also Joseph Campbell, *The Hero with a Thousand Faces* (New York: Meridian Books, 1956; first edition, New York: Pantheon Books, 1949).

18. See Michel Gresset's comments on the sexual symbolism of the river scene in *Dictionnaire des Oeuvres Contemporaines* (Paris: Laffont-Bompiani, 1968), pp. 693–94. Referring to Sandor Ferenczi's essay on "The Symbolism of the Bridge" (*Further Contributions to the Theory and Technique of Psycho-analysis,* New York: Basic Books, 1952, pp. 352–56), Gresset points out that while the mother is represented both by the river to be crossed and by the landscape to be reached, the bridge may be equated with the father's penis. The whole river scene could thus be interpreted as a symbolic representation of the fertilization of the womb. As Gresset observes, this interpretation is borne out by the farmers' talk about the bridge reported by Tull (cf. p. 83): the first man to cross it was doctor Peabody, when he was called by Uncle Billy to deliver his wife. However, the interesting point is the fact that the bridge has been washed away by the flooded river—another reminder of male impotency in the novel.

19. Freud, Ernest Jones, Otto Rank, and others have commented upon the fact that in dreams, as in mythology and initiation rites, the delivery of a child from the uterine waters is commonly represented, by way of distortion, as the entry of the child into water. See especially Sigmund Freud's *Interpretation of Dreams* (*The Basic Writings of Sigmund Freud,* New York: The Modern Library, 1938, pp. 394–95) and Otto Rank, *The Myth of the Birth of the Hero* (New York: Robert Brunner, 1952). For further comment on the birth symbolism of the river scene, see Melvin Backman, *Faulkner: The Major Years* (Bloomington: Indiana University Press, 1966), pp. 63–64. Backman points out that "the action of the scene stops in one place as Darl and Cash recall the birth of Jewel." He sees "some vague parallels between the river and the womb: for example, the way in which Cash is delivered from the water may suggest a kind of rebirth."

20. "Address upon receiving the Nobel Prize for Literature," in *Essays, Speeches and Public Letters by William Faulkner,* ed. James B. Meriwether (New York: Random House, 1966), p. 120.

21. See Olga W. Vickery, *The Novels of William Faulkner* (Baton Rouge: Louisiana State University Press, 1959), p. 52.

22. See *FU*, p. 111.

23. The first critic to analyze the meaning of Darl's laughter was John K. Simon in "What Are You Laughing At, Darl?: Madness and

Humor in *As I Lay Dying,*" *College English,* XXV (November 1963) 104–10.

24. Michel Foucault, *Histoire de la Folie* (Paris: Plon, 1961), p. 19. A translation of Foucault's book has been published under the title *Madness and Civilization: A History of Insanity in the Age of Reason,* trans. R. Howard (New York: Pantheon, 1965) ; see p. 16.

25. See, e.g., Maurice E. Coindreau, "Le Puritanisme de William Faulkner," *Cahiers du Sud,* XXII (April 1935), 266–67.

26. Howard, p. 16.

27. Søren Kierkegaard, *Concluding Unscientific Postscript,* trans. David F. Swenson and Walter Lowrie (Princeton: Princeton University Press, 1941), p. 175.

28. The Faulknerian concept of "astonishment" appears as a kind of tragic inversion of the sense of wonder, whose importance in American literature has been shown by Tony Tanner in *The Reign of Wonder* (New York: Harper & Row, 1967).

29. See *FU,* p. 112.

30. Calvin Bedient, "Pride and Nakedness: *As I Lay Dying,*" *Modern Language Quarterly,* XXIX (March 1968), 62.

31. Ibid.

32. These questions were raised by many writers of Faulkner's generation. In America, suspicion of language was particularly strong after World War I and came as a reaction to the cheap rhetoric of the Wilson era. In their early works, T.S. Eliot and Hemingway, for instance, express a distrust of abstractions and generalities very similar to Faulkner's. See Floyd C. Watkins, *The Flesh and the Word* (Nashville: Vanderbilt University Press, 1971), especially pp. 3–10.

33. *Mosquitoes* (New York: Liveright, 1927), p. 130.

34. Ibid., p. 186.

35. *Absalom, Absalom!* (New York: Random House, 1936), p. 251.

36. "Address upon receiving the Nobel Prize for Literature," p. 120.

8. Critical Reception

1. See Alan Reynolds Thompson, "The Cult of Cruelty," *The Bookman,* LXXIV (January-February 1932), 477–87.

2. For a general study of Faulkner's critical reception in America,

see Frederick J. Hoffman, "An Introduction," in *William Faulkner: Three Decades of Criticism,* ed. Frederick J. Hoffman and Olga W. Vickery (East Lansing: Michigan State University Press, 1960), pp. 1–50.

3. Granville Hicks, "The Past and Future of William Faulkner," *The Bookman* LXXIV (September 1931), 17–24.

4. "A Witch's Brew: *As I Lay Dying,*" *The New York Times Book Review* (October 19, 1930), 6.

5. Clifton Fadiman, "Morbidity in Fiction," *The Nation,* CXXXI (November 5, 1930), 500–501. Reprinted in Clifton Fadiman, "William Faulkner," *Party of One* (Cleveland: World Publishing Company, 1955), pp. 98–99, 102–104.

6. Kenneth White, *The New Republic,* LXV (November 19, 1930) ,27.

7. See Carvel Collins, "About the Sketches," in *William Faulkner: New Orleans Sketches* (New Brunswick, N.J.: Rutgers University Press, 1958), pp. 9–34.

8. J.K.W.B., "Literature and Less," *Times-Picayune,* October 26, 1930, 33. Quoted by O.B. Emerson in "Prophet Next Door," *Reality and Myth: Essays in American Literature in Memory of Richmond Croom Beatty,* ed. E. Walker and Robert L. Welker (Nashville: Vanderbilt University Press, 1964), pp. 245–46.

9. See Gordon Price-Stephens, "The British Reception of William Faulkner—1929–1962," *Mississippi Quarterly, XVIII* (Summer 1965), 119–200.

10. Edwin Muir, *The Listener, XIV* (October 16, 1935), 681.

11. Howard Spring, *Evening Standard,* September 26, 1935.

12. Philip Henderson, *The Novel Today: Studies in Contemporary Attitudes* (London: John Lane, 1936), pp. 147–50.

13. *As I Lay Dying* was the second of Faulkner's novels to appear in France, *Sanctuary* having been published in 1933. See Maurice Edgar Coindreau, "William Faulkner in France," *Yale French Studies,* no. 10 (Autumn 1952), 85–91, especially 87–88.

14. M. E. Coindreau, "William Faulkner," *Nouvelle Revue Française, XXXVI* (June 1931), 926.

15. Valéry Larbaud, Préface, *Tandis que j'agonise* (Paris: Gallimard, 1934), p. I.

16. Ibid., pp. II–III.

17. Marcel Thiébaut, *Revue de Paris, July* 15, 1934, 474.

18. See Eugène Dabit, *Europe,* October 15, 1934, 294–96.

19. The phrase ("l'allure d'une grande fresque lyrique") is from J. Lassaigne in *Revue mondiale,* July 1, 1934, 32.

20. Dabit, trans. M. E. Coindreau, in "William Faulkner in France," 89. We have taken the liberty of inserting two words *(obstinate, bizarre)* omitted in Coindreau's translation.

21. Ibid.

22. In July 1964, the Dallas Theater Center presented *Journey to Jefferson,* a more traditional adaptation by Robert L. Flynn, at the Théâtre des Nations. It is worth recalling too that in 1949 *As I Lay Dying* was adapted into dance by Valerie Bettis. See Truman Capote's review, "Faulkner Dances," in *Theatre Arts, XXXIII* (April 1949), 49.

23. See Jean-Louis Barrault, *Réflexions sur le théâtre* (Paris: Jacques Vautrain, 1949), pp. 41–53.

24. Antonin Artaud, "Un Spectacle magique," *Nouvelle Revue Française,* XLV (July 1935), 136–38. Reprinted in *Cahiers de la Compagnie Madeleine Renaud-J.-L. Barrault,* II, 7ème cahier (Paris: Julliard, 1954), 39–42.

25. *Réflexions sur le théâtre,* p. 49.

26. *Carrefour,* November 14, 1950. For a study of the critical reception of Faulkner in France and an assessment of his influence on French literature, see Stanley D. Woodworth, *William Faulkner en France* (1931–1952), Collection "Situation," no. 2 (Paris: M. J. Minard, Lettres Modernes, 1959).

27. George Marion O'Donnell, "Faulkner's Mythology," *Three Decades of Criticism,* p. 82. This essay was first published in *The Kenyon Review,* I (Summer 1939), 285–99.

28. Ibid., p. 87.

29. Ibid.

30. Robert Penn Warren, "William Faulkner," *Three Decades of Criticism,* p. 119. Warren's article had first appeared under the title "Cowley's Faulkner," in *The New Republic,* CXV (August 12, 1946), 176–80; (August 26, 1946), 234–37.

31. Cleanth Brooks, *William Faulkner: The Yoknapatawpha Country* (New Haven: Yale University Press, 1963), pp. 142–43.

32. See his comments on the episode with Jewel and the stranger, ibid., pp. 143–44.

33. Ibid., p. 166.

34. Irving Howe, *William Faulkner,* 2nd edition, rev. (New York: Vintage Books, 1962), p. 189.

35. Ibid.

36. Melvin Backman, *Faulkner: The Major Years* (Bloomington: Indiana University Press, 1966), p. 177.

37. Walter Brylowski, *Faulkner's Olympian Laugh* (Detroit: Wayne State University Press, 1968, p. 86.

38. Olga W. Vickery, *"As I Lay Dying,"* *Perspective*, III (Autumn 1950), 179–91. Reprinted in a slightly revised form and under a different title ("The Dimensions of Consciousness: *As I Lay Dying*") in *The Novels of William Faulkner*, pp. 50–65; and in *Three Decades of Criticism*, pp. 232–47.

39. *The Novels of William Faulkner*, p. 52.

40. See Edward Wasiolek, *"As I Lay Dying:* Distortion in the Slow Eddy of Current Opinion," *Critique*, III (Spring-Fall 1959), 15–23.

41. Ibid., 23.

42. Edmond L. Volpe, *A Reader's Guide to William Faulkner* (New York: Noonday Press, 1964), p. 126.

43. Ibid., p. 128.

44. See *FU*, p. 112.

45. See *FU*, p. 114.

46. *LG*, p. 254.

BIBLIOGRAPHY

I. EARLY REVIEWS

American:

Anonymous. "A Witch's Brew: *As I Lay Dying.*" *New York Times Book Review,* October 19, 1930, 6.

B., J.K.W. "Literature and Less." *Times-Picayune,* October 26, 1930, 33.

Davenport, Basil. "In the Mire." *Saturday Review of Literature,* VII (November 22, 1930), 362.

Dawson, Margaret Cheney. "Beside Addie's Coffin." *New York Herald Tribune,* October 5, 1930, sect. XI, 6.

Fadiman, Clifton. "Morbidity in Fiction." *The Nation,* CXXXI (November 5, 1930), 500.

Hicks, Granville. "The Past and Future of William Faulkner." *The Bookman, LXXIV* (September 1931), 17–24.

Josephson, Matthew. "The Younger Generation: Its Young Novelists." *Virginia Quarterly Review,* IX (April 1933), 250–253.

Smith, Harrison. "A Troubled Vision: *As I Lay Dying.*" *Southwest Review,* XVI (January 1931), 16–17.

Wade, John D. "The South in Its Fiction." *Virginia Quarterly Review,* VII (January 1931), 125–26.

White, Kenneth. *"As I Lay Dying,* by William Faulkner." *The New Republic,* LXV (November 19, 1930), 27.

British:

Anonymous. *The London Mercury,* XXXIII (November 1935), 89.

Anonymous. *The Times,* September 27, 1935.

Anonymous. *The Times Literary Supplement,* no. 1756 (September 26, 1935), 594.

B., H. *The Manchester Guardian,* October 4, 1935.

Blakestone, Oswell. *Life and Letters Today,* XIII (December 1935), 198.

BIBLIOGRAPHY

Brophy, John. *Time and Tide,* XVI (October 19, 1935), 1489–91.
Gould, Gerald. *The Observer,* September 29, 1935.
Jones, E.B.C. *The Adelphi,* XI (February 1936), 316–18.
Macmillan, A. *The Scottish Standard,* I (November 1935), 28.
Muir, Edwin. *The Listener,* XIV (October 16, 1935), 681.
O'Faolain, Sean. *The Fortnightly,* CXXXVIII (December 1935), 637–38.
Quennell, Peter. *The New Statesman and Nation,* X (October 5, 1935), 453–54.
Spring, Howard. *Evening Standard,* September 26, 1935.

French:

Dabit, Eugène. *Europe,* October 15, 1934, 294.
Lassaigne, J. *Revue Mondiale,* July 1, 1934, 32.
Le Breton, Maurice. *Revue anglo-américaine,* XIII (June 1936), 471.
Thiébaut, Marcel. *Revue de Paris,* XLI (July 15, 1934), 474–76.
Toesca, Maurice. *Gazette des Lettres,* January 18, 1947, 9.

II. CRITICAL STUDIES

Adams, Richard P. *Faulkner: Myth and Motion.* Princeton, N.J.: Princeton University Press, 1968, pp. 71–84. Relates *As I Lay Dying* to mythic death-and-rebirth patterns and defines the novel as a kind of pastoral elegy.
Backman, Melvin. *Faulkner: The Major Years.* Bloomington: Indiana University Press, 1966), pp. 50–66. Perceptive comments on the novel's symbolism, but the general interpretation ("a work illumined by nascent faith in humanity") is excessively optimistic.
Bedient, Calvin. "Pride and Nakedness: *As I Lay Dying.*" *Modern Language Quarterly,* XXIX (March 1968), 61–76. The most brilliant and most original essay on *As I Lay Dying* since Olga W. Vickery's. Analyzes the novel in the light of two of its key concepts —*pride* and *nakedness.* Penetrating insights into Darl and Cash.
Beidler, Peter G. "Faulkner's Techniques of Characterization: Jewel in *As I Lay Dying.*" *Etudes Anglaises,* XXI (July-September 1968), 236–42. A careful scrutiny of the novelist's method of characterization, exemplified by Faulkner's portrayal of Jewel.
Blotner, Joseph L. *"As I Lay Dying:* Christian Lore and Irony." *Twen-*

tieth Century Literature, III (April 1957), 14–19. Points out Christian and particularly biblical parallels (the Flood and the Noah story), and their ironical use by Faulkner.

Bradford, M. E. "Addie Bundren and the Design of *As I Lay Dying.*" *The Southern Review,* VI (Autumn 1970), 1093–99. Discusses Addie's central role as "the auditor of all the reveries which go into that account of her decline, death, funeral journey, and related events. . . ."

Bridgman, Richard. "As Hester Prynne Lay Dying." *English Language Notes,* II (June 1965), 294–96. *The Scarlet Letter* as source for *As I Lay Dying.*

Brooks, Cleanth. "Odyssey of the Bundrens." In *William Faulkner: The Yoknapatawpha Country.* New Haven: Yale University Press, 1963, pp. 141–66. Excellent chapter on *As I Lay Dying.* Shrewd and stimulating analyses of the characters. Makes the strongest case for the heroism of the Bundrens.

Brylowski, Walter. "The Comic Vision." In *Faulkner's Olympian Laugh: Myth in the Novels.* Detroit: Wayne State University Press, 1968, pp. 86–96. Examines Faulkner's "mythic mode of thought" and interprets *As I Lay Dying* as an expression of his "comic vision."

Campbell, Harry M. "Experiment and Achievement: *As I Lay Dying* and *The Sound and the Fury.*" *Sewanee Review,* LI (April 1943), 305–20. Sees in the novel "little more than a light framework hastily thrown together to justify unmotivated Tourneurian eloquence."

Collins, Carvel. "The Pairing of *The Sound and the Fury* and *As I Lay Dying.*" *Princeton University Library Chronicle,* XVIII (Spring 1957), 114–23. Points out thematic and structural similarities between *The Sound and the Fury* and *As I Lay Dying,* and investigates the mythic patterns underlying both novels. According to Collins, *As I Lay Dying* offers parallels with Greek mythology; there are close correspondences between Demeter-Persephone-Kore and Addie-Dewey Dell-Cora. An ingenious but often questionable essay, which inspired several other critics.

Cross, Barbara M. "Apocalypse and Comedy in *As I Lay Dying.*" *Texas Studies in Literature,* III (Summer 1961), 251–58. Discusses "the ironic interplay of low comedy and apocalyptic fervor." Another mythological reading, marred by many inaccuracies.

Dickerson, Mary Jane. *"As I Lay Dying* and 'The Waste Land'—Some Relationships." *Mississippi Quarterly,* XVII (Summer 1964), 129–

35. Explores the similarities between T.S. Eliot's poem and Faulkner's novel.

Dickerson, Mary Jane. "Some Sources of Faulkner's Myth in *As I Lay Dying." Mississippi Quarterly,* XIX (Summer 1966), 132–42. Another attempt to establish Faulkner's mythical frame of reference, with particular emphasis on vegetation myths.

Ditsky, John. "Faulkner's Carousel: Point of View in *As I Lay Dying." Laurel Review,* X (Spring 1970), 74–85. A general essay with a misleading title: Faulkner's use of multiple point of view is cursorily dealt with; despite the aptness of the carousel metaphor, the author fails to provide new insights into Faulkner's narrative method.

Douglas, Harold J., and Robert Daniel. "Faulkner and the Puritanism of the South." *Tennessee Studies in Literature,* II (1957), 1–13. Contends that *As I Lay Dying* "resembles *The Scarlet Letter* in ways that virtually establish a direct influence."

Franklin, Rosemary. "Animal Magnetism in *As I Lay Dying." American Quarterly,* XVIII (Spring 1966), 24–34. An interesting commentary on the meaning of Cash's reference to "animal magnetism" and on the role of extrasensory phenomena in the novel.

Franklin, R. W. "Narrative Management in *As I Lay Dying." Modern Fiction Studies,* XIII (Spring 1967), 57–65. A methodical investigation of Faulkner's narrative technique. Examines the difficulties involved in the use of the present tense and points up Faulkner's inconsistencies in the handling of his narrative mode.

Friedman, Melvin J. "Le Monologue intérieur dans *As I Lay Dying." Revue des Lettres Modernes,* V (Winter 1958–1959), 331–44. Studies the differentiation of interior monologue according to character and compares Faulkner's use of the stream-of-consciousness technique with Virginia Woolf's in *The Waves.*

Garrett, George Palmer. "Some Revisions in *As I Lay Dying." Modern Language Notes,* LXXIII (June 1958), 414–17. An examination of Faulkner's revisions, based on evidence from the first and last manuscript page.

Goellner, Jack Gordon. "A Closer Look at *As I Lay Dying." Perspective,* VII (Spring 1954), 42–54. Rejects the heroic interpretation of the novel and argues that its meaning is to be sought "within the psychology of the Bundren kinship, in the tangled web of sympathetic and conflicting relationships which provide inseparably the form and content of *As I Lay Dying.*"

Handy, William J. "*As I Lay Dying:* Faulkner's Inner Reporter." *Kenyon Review,* XXI (Summer 1959), 437–51. One of the first articles to recognize the importance of Darl. Distinguishes "the Darl of action and event" and "the Darl of inner consciousness."

Hemenway, Robert. "Enigmas of Being in *As I Lay Dying.*" *Modern Fiction Studies,* XVI (Summer 1970), 133–46. A close reading of Darl's reverie on sleep, being, and nonbeing.

Hoffman, Frederick J. *William Faulkner.* New York: Twayne Publishers, 1961, pp. 60–65. Sees the essence of the novel in the tensions between Darl and Jewel.

Howe, Irving. *William Faulkner: A Critical Study,* second edition. New York: Vintage Books, 1962, pp. 52–56, 175–91. Overemphasizes the sympathetic rendering of the novel's characters. Howe's is by far the coziest view of the book: "Of all Faulkner's novels, *As I Lay Dying* is the warmest, the kindliest and most affectionate."

Howell, Elmo. "Faulkner's Jumblies: The Nonsense World of *As I Lay Dying.*" *Arizona Quarterly,* XVI (Spring 1960), 70–78. Compares the Bundrens to Edward Lear's "Jumblies" and considers the novel primarily a nonsense story.

Humphrey, Robert. *Stream of Consciousness in the Modern Novel.* Berkeley: University of California Press, 1954, pp. 20–21, 36–37, 64–65, 67, 72–73, 104–106. On the place of *As I Lay Dying* in the development of the stream-of-consciousness novel. Some very pertinent remarks on the importance of figures of speech in one of the Dewey Dell sections.

Kerr, Elizabeth M. "*As I Lay Dying* as Ironic Quest." *Wisconsin Studies in Contemporary Literature,* III (Winter 1962), 5–19. Interpretation of *As I Lay Dying* as an ironic inversion of the traditional quest romance.

King, Roma, Jr. "The Janus Symbol in *As I Lay Dying.*" *University of Kansas City Review,* XXI (June 1955), 287–90. Regards the horse and the fish as the two complementary faces of the same symbol, the former representing passion, power, and life, the latter suggesting death. An unwarranted simplification of Faulkner's symbolism.

Kirk, Robert W. "Faulkner's Anse Bundren." *Georgia Review,* XIX (Winter 1965), 446–52. Claims that Anse is the central figure of the novel; stresses the comic features of the character and glosses over his essential baseness.

Le Breton, Maurice. "Le Thème de la vie et de la mort dans *As I Lay*

Dying." *Revue des Lettres Modernes,* V (Winter 1958–1959), 516–54. Discusses the relationships between being, not-being, and the nature of the self, as presented through the main characters. A finely balanced essay, which provides judicious insights into the thematics of the novel.

Mellard, James M. "Faulkner's Philosophical Novel: Ontological Themes in *As I Lay Dying.*" *The Personalist,* XLVIII (Autumn 1967), 509–23. Considers *As I Lay Dying* "the most philosophically versatile work in the Faulkner canon," and analyzes it as an illustration of three metaphysical attitudes: nominalism (Addie), idealism (Darl), and realism (Cash). A new and most rewarding approach to the novel.

Millgate, Michael. *The Achievement of William Faulkner.* New York: Random House, 1966, pp. 104–12. A rather brief but interesting chapter on *As I Lay Dying,* with very useful information on the genesis of the novel.

O'Connor, William Van. *The Tangled Fire of William Faulkner.* Minneapolis: University of Minnesota Press, 1954, pp. 45–53. Considers "the obligation to be involved" as the major theme of the book.

O'Donnell, George Marion. "Faulkner's Mythology." *Kenyon Review,* I (Summer 1939), 285–99. The first interpretation of the novel in terms of heroism and traditional morality.

Parsons, Thornton H. "Doing the Best They Can." *Georgia Review,* XXIII (Fall 1969), 292–306. Argues that the family unity is the overriding norm of the novel.

Randall, Julia. "Some Notes on *As I Lay Dying.*" *Hopkins Review,* IV (Summer 1951), 47–51. Has perceptive remarks on Faulkner's technique and art, but careful reading of the novel does not bear out the author's thesis that the present of the narrative is merely a past relived by memory.

Reaver, J. Russell. "This Vessel of Clay: A Thematic Comparison of Faulkner's *As I Lay Dying* and Latorre's *The Old Woman of Peralillo.*" *Florida State University Studies,* no. 14 (1954), 131–40. On the theme of the unburiable corpse.

Roberts, J. L. "The Individual and the Family: Faulkner's *As I Lay Dying.*" *Arizona Quarterly,* XVI (Spring 1960), 26–38. Thoroughly mistaken about several characters: Dewey Dell is described as an obtuse egoist, Vardaman as mentally retarded, and Darl as a paragon of sanity.

Rossky, William. "*As I Lay Dying*: The Insane World." *Texas Studies in Literature and Language,* IV (Spring 1962), 87–95. Stresses the comedy of the absurd and the quixotic nature of the Bundrens' journey.

Sadler, David F. "The Second Mrs. Bundren: Another Look at the Ending of *As I Lay Dying.*" *American Literature,* XXXVII (March 1965), 65–69. Contends that in acquiring his new wife Anse dispenses with the wedding; interprets the ending as the rejection of Addie's values by the Bundrens.

Sanderlin, Robert Reed. "*As I Lay Dying:* Christian Symbols and Thematic Implications." *Southern Quarterly,* VII (January 1969), 155–66. Maintains that "the theme of judgment is the integrating principle which helps to tie the various religious symbols together"; takes up the mistaken notion of Cash's moral growth during the journey.

Sawyer, Kenneth B. "Hero in *As I Lay Dying.*" *Faulkner Studies,* III (Summer-Autumn, 1954), 30–33. Regards Jewel as the motive force of the novel and as the only character to achieve tragic proportions.

Simon, John K. " 'What Are You Laughing At, Darl?': Madness and Humor in *As I Lay Dying.*" *College English,* XXV (November 1963), 104–10. Shows the significance of Darl as a pivotal figure in the novel and the relevance of his madness to its thematic development. A provocative essay, with many fresh insights into the book.

———. "The Scene and the Imagery of Metamorphosis in *As I Lay Dying.*" *Criticism,* VII (Winter 1965), 1–22. The first article devoted to the setting of the novel, with emphasis on the themes of metamorphosis and the Apocalypse.

Slabey, Robert M. "*As I Lay Dying* as an Existential Novel." *Bucknell Review,* XI (December 1963), 12–23. Calls attention to the existential aspects of the novel and to the affinities between Faulkner's vision and Sartre's philosophy. But Slabey is wrong in defining *As I Lay Dying* as "a picture of meaninglessness," and in equating existentialism with nihilism.

Slatoff, Walter J. *Quest for Failure.* Ithaca, N.Y.: Cornell University Press, 1960, pp. 158–73. Stresses the unresolved tensions and irreducible ambiguities to be found in the novel.

Stallman, R. W. "A Cryptogram: *As I Lay Dying.*" In *The Houses that James Built.* East Lansing: Michigan State University Press,

1961, pp. 200–11. A stimulating but sometimes overingenious study of the novel's symbolism.

Stonesifer, Richard J. "In Defense of Dewey Dell." *Educational Leader*, XXII (July 1, 1958), 27–33. Judicious rehabilitation of Dewey Dell, a character neglected or misunderstood by most critics.

Sutherland, Ronald. *"As I Lay Dying: A Faulkner Microcosm."* *Queen's Quarterly*, LXXIII (Winter 1966), 541–49. An examination of Faulkner's variations in style. Ranks *As I Lay Dying* among the novelist's "most fundamental achievements."

Swiggart, Peter. "A Modern Mock-Epic." In *The Art of Faulkner's Novels.* (Austin: University of Texas Press, 1962, 108–30. Good chapter on *As I Lay Dying,* focusing on the theme of "human rage directed against a personified concept of time."

Vickery, Olga W. *"As I Lay Dying."* *Perspective,* III (Autumn 1950), 179–91. Reprinted in Hoffman, Frederick J., and Olga W. Vickery, eds., *William Faulkner: Two Decades of Criticism* (East Lansing: Michigan State College Press, 1951), pp. 189–205, and, in a slightly different version, in the author's book, *The Novels of William Faulkner: A Critical Interpretation* (Baton Rouge: Louisiana State University Press, 1959 and 1964), pp. 50–65, and in Hoffman, Frederick J., and Olga W. Vickery, eds., *William Faulkner: Three Decades of Criticism* (Michigan State University Press, 1960), pp. 232–47. Vickery's essay was the first to pay attention to the close links between structure, theme, and psychology, and to analyze the novel in terms of kinship. Although questionable on minor points, it provides a careful, sensitive, and extremely intelligent reading of *As I Lay Dying,* and remains to date one of the very best written on this book.

Volpe, Edmond L. *A Reader's Guide to William Faulkner.* New York: Noonday Press, 1964, pp. 126–40, 377–82. Another "absurdist" interpretation of the novel, reducing its meaning to a grim joke.

Waggoner, Hyatt H. "Vision." In *William Faulkner: From Jefferson to the World.* Lexington: University of Kentucky Press, 1959, pp. 62–87. The most Christian interpretation. According to Waggoner, *As I Lay Dying* "asserts the emotional and imaginative, but not the logical, validity of Biblical and Christian symbolism."

Wasiolek, Edward. *"As I Lay Dying:* Distortion in the Slow Eddy of Current Opinion." *Critique,* III (Spring–Fall 1959), 15–23. Takes issue with the humanistic-heroic interpretation, but weakens his argument by exaggerating the bitterness of Faulkner's irony.

Watkins, Floyd C. "The Word and the Deed in Faulkner's First Great Novels." In *The Flesh and the Word*. Nashville: Vanderbilt University Press, 1971, pp. 181–202. An analysis of the relationship between language and reality in *The Sound and the Fury, As I Lay Dying,* and *Sanctuary*.

Watkins, Floyd C., and William B. Dillingham. "The Mind of Vardaman." *Philological Quarterly*, XXXIX (April 1960), 247–51. Refutes the idea that Vardaman is an idiot.

Williams, Ora G. "The Theme of Endurance in *As I Lay Dying*." *Louisiana Studies,* IX (Summer 1970), 100–104. Attempts to show that the Bundrens exemplify the qualities Faulkner praised in his Nobel Prize Speech.

INDEX